THIS
OUR EXILE

Mark Raper SJ, courtesy JRS

THIS
OUR EXILE

A Spiritual Journey
with the Refugees of East Africa

James Martin SJ

FOREWORD BY ROBERT COLES

ORBIS BOOKS

Maryknoll, New York 10545

Designed by Elizabeth O'Keefe

Manufactured in the United States of America

Imprimi Potest:
The Very Rev. Robert J. Levens, S.J.
Provincial, The Society of Jesus
New England Province

Martin, James, S.J.
     This our exile : a spiritual journey with the refugees in East Africa / James Martin : foreword by Robert Coles.
        p.   cm.
     ISBN 1-57075-250-8 (paper)
     1. Martin, James, S.J.   2. Jesuits—Missions—Kenya—Nairobi.
3. Missionaries—Kenya—Nairobi—Biography.   4. Missionaries—United States—Biography.   5. Church work with refugees—Kenya—Nairobi.
6. Jesuit Refugee Service. Eastern Africa Regional Office—Biography.
I. Title.
BV3532.M35A3   1999
276.762'50829—dc21   98-43648
                                                              CIP

Mwamini Mungi si mtovu.
Who trusts in God lacks nothing.
—Swahili proverb

For the refugees

CONTENTS

•

FOREWORD

by Robert Coles

BY LEAVING A WORLD we've learned to know all our lives for another, far distant, and far different one, we have a chance not only to explore new terrain, new versions of humanity, but also (through the help of those so unlike us in certain respects) to catch sight of ourselves in ways otherwise denied us; and thereby we get, as Graham Greene reminded us, to "the heart of the matter." It is well and appropriate that James Martin, a young Jesuit, quotes Greene at one point in his account of a seminarian's work of service in Africa. Greene was himself a Catholic who constantly drew on his faith as he wrote his novels, and he was also a life-long traveler who understood so well the way a literal distance from one's usual routines, one's familiar circumstances, can give one a kind of psychological and moral distance upon oneself, a sense of perspective otherwise not readily available.

In the pages ahead a young, thoughtful American of earnest good will tells us his African experiences with a novelist's sensibility: a fine sense of detail, a narrative energy, a capacity to evoke character, to portray human variety and complexity. But this is not yet another chronicle of travel through a continent that most of us in America will never get to see. Nor is it a traditional exercise in religious piety—a missionary tale, as it were, meant to boost the reader's spirituality. Rather, Mr. Martin aims to bring us closer, again, to "the heart of the matter"—to our common vulnerability, wherever we are: that is, our shared knowledge that we are here only for a while, a fate that no acquisition of money and power will change. That being the case, those who go to be of medical (or yes, spiritual) assistance to others, seemingly so worse off by dint of extreme poverty, soon enough are caught off balance; the afflicted are not without their own substantial dignity—to the point that the "mission" of the visitor, the healer, or teacher, is to take personal notice, realize how much there is to learn from these people so readily regarded as needy, impoverished, uneducated, with few or no prospects.

The heart of the Christian message is its relentless, unyielding (and quite revolutionary) insistence on a topsy-turvy view of things—as in "the last shall be first, the first last." Again and again the traveling, observant Jesus, intent on teaching and healing, favored the ironic, even paradoxical, moral fable. He told story after story that reminded his listeners (and today, those attend him, as readers of the Bible) that the apparent may not be real, that there is more to this world than meets the casual eye, that those who have known hurt and pain and jeopardy of various kinds have, often enough, learned lessons from this life that are denied the rest of us; and that, indeed, to have known privilege and more privilege of various kinds is to have been exposed to a great deal of moral jeopardy: the smugness and provinciality one sees not rarely among all too many of us who consider ourselves lucky to be *here*, not *there*, living this kind of life rather than that kind.

Graham Greene knew quite well that the "heart of the matter" is our common humanity, no matter who we are, and where we call home. Put differently, sometimes we have to leave home to find home—leave our lives to find them, with the help of others. James Martin's book tells us that—well, really shows us that—through incident after incident, carefully and lovingly rendered; his Africa is yet another place that has received pilgrims, anxious not only to travel through a particular countryside but also upward, on their way to God's gracious presence.

Don Doll SJ

Before arriving in Kenya, when I thought of Africa I pictured only scenes like this one, in the Maasai Mara National Park. My understanding of the region would soon change—quickly, and in unexpected ways.

INTRODUCTION:
INTO AFRICA

Kuitwa ni kutumwa.
To be called is to be sent.
—Swahili proverb

RECENTLY, I SPENT two years in Kenya working with refugees from across East Africa. I was there with the Jesuit Refugee Service, a Catholic relief organization. My assignment was to help refugees—who had come from Somalia, Rwanda, Burundi, Uganda, Ethiopia, Eritrea, Sudan, Mozambique, and Liberia—start small businesses, or, in the antiseptic lingo of relief agencies, "income-generating activities." My two years ran from 1992 through 1994, and so I lived in East Africa during the time of both the famine in Somalia and the genocide in Rwanda. My time saw not only dramatically increased flows of refugees into the dry Kenyan countryside, but also an awakened interest on the part of the West in the problems and concerns of East Africa.

I should say right away that I had never planned on working in Africa. Unlike a close friend who, when I told her of my assignment, clapped her hands and said, "Wow! I've always wanted to go to Africa!" I pretty much *never* wanted to go to Africa. Granted, I'm a sucker for all of those nature specials on TV, had seen *Out of Africa* a few times, and more or less followed what had been going on in the continent (less rather than more); but like most Americans, I was not particularly interested in going there. Too dangerous, too dirty and too far. And if I were planning a random two-year stay away from home, I'd just as soon have picked somewhere in Western Europe. Paris or Rome would have been just fine, thanks.

As for working with refugees, I never imagined myself cast in the role of those aid workers one sees on television, handing out food from the backs of trucks in refugee camps. While I saw it as an undeniably good thing to do, I was, in a word, too frightened to envision myself doing anything remotely like that in a place so far away.

So how did I end up in Africa? The short answer is that I was sent. The two-year assignment in Nairobi was to be part of my training as a Jesuit.

A little background: The Jesuits, a Catholic religious order, ask their members to undergo a rather lengthy process of training—ten or eleven years in all. Following a two-year stint studying philosophy, and prior to four years of theology, a Jesuit sets aside his books to work full-time for a few years. Some American Jesuits spend this period teaching in high schools or universities, as did many of my friends. Others work in parishes or retreat houses. Others work in what are still called, in that decidedly loaded term, the "missions."

So, toward the end of my philosophy studies I was asked to consider what type of work I might like to do. At first I thought I would prefer to work in the United States. Two years earlier I had spent some time as a Jesuit novice working with the poor in Jamaica, which I found quite difficult: the whine and bite of mosquitoes waking you up in the early dawn, enormous lizards crawling around the shower stall, and all the rest. So while I liked the idea of working with the needy, the notion of returning to the developing world initially held little appeal. Besides, I thought, there were plenty of poor people in the States—why go halfway across the world?

Around this time, though, I began to hear more and more about an international group of Jesuits who worked with refugees.

Shortly before suffering a debilitating stroke in 1980, Pedro Arrupe, the Jesuit general superior, aware of the exploding refugee populations across the globe, had an idea. Arrupe realized that, simply put, there were Jesuits everywhere in the world, and there were refugees everywhere in the world. Why not bring the two together? Following the advice of St. Ignatius of Loyola, the founder of the Society of Jesus, who stressed the value of going where there was the "greatest need," Arrupe created the Jesuit Refugee Service (JRS).

It seemed that I ran across articles about JRS weekly. (Of course, almost any reading was more interesting than Kant or Heidegger.) The more I read the more it seemed to me that *this* was what I should do next. And the more I considered the possibility, the more the bothersome physical problems—bugs, lizards, water, health, whatever—faded into the background, leaving behind only a desire to work with the poor.

Part of the allure, I admit, had to do with a sense of adventure as well as what could accurately be termed pride. I thought that working with refugees was the most difficult, the most impressive, or, in other words, the *coolest* ministry you could do—admittedly not the noblest reason to journey halfway across the world.

Still, the main reason was a real desire to help the poor. Besides, it was only two years. How difficult could it be?

JRS told me of three spots where they most needed help: Southeast Asia, Central America, and Africa. Did I have a preference? Not really, I said. Where did they need me the most?

As it turned out, the Jesuits in Nairobi, Kenya, the headquarters for the refugee team in East Africa, needed help with the running of small refugee businesses. That sounded promising. Before I entered the Jesuits I had graduated from business school and worked in the corporate world for six years. Perhaps I could put my long dormant finance and accounting skills to good use. Fortunately, there would be another young American Jesuit working and living with me in the local Jesuit community. And since Nairobi was a big city, my fears about health and the other physical annoyances were for the moment assuaged.

Predictably, my friends and family were shocked when I told them of my decision. My parents, in point of fact, hit the roof. When I entered the Jesuits they were terrified they wouldn't see me as frequently as they wanted to, thinking back to times in their youth when priests and nuns were almost entirely cut off from their families. But I had reassured them. "Don't worry," I actually said when I entered the novitiate, "It's not like I'm going to be sent to *Africa* or anything." On the other hand, my friends, even those who were not particularly religious, saw the possibility of a stint in Africa as a type of "good works" and were able to evince more excitement about my assignment.

So I went. And nothing was as I expected it. And my life changed totally.

It's probably simplest to say that I was changed through a simple concatenation of events: I saw this, I did this, I met this person. And that would be true. The things I saw and heard and did created a different person, by virtue of a host of new sights and sounds that now float around in my head. All of that I expected: I expected to meet people with unusual backgrounds and have a few exotic adventures. But that would be only part of the story.

The other part of the story is how my heart was changed.

The refugees in East Africa, people whom I had only read about in newspapers, people whose lives I (literally) couldn't begin to imagine, transformed my heart in ways that I also couldn't have imagined. Their lives, a full measure of sorrows and joys, forced me to confront the basic human questions of what it means to suffer pain and to experience happiness. Seeing how the lives of the refugees continually moved between the twin poles of despair and hope showed me what enables people to continue, despite incredible difficulties, and still believe in a good God. Or, as one redoubtable Rwandese woman (whom you will soon meet) would tell me, "God is very good!" Their magnificent openness to life helped me face my own difficulties more honestly, and to stay in Kenya despite some strong temptations to leave. Most especially, in coming to know the refugees, and in being invited into their lives, I came to know more fully what it means to love and be loved.

And that's what this book is about. It's a simple story, centering around my work with the refugees in trying to help them earn a living. Actually, it's a series of stories, some funny, some almost unbearably sad, some frankly incredible, and some that are difficult to categorize. The centerpiece of the book is the lives and stories of the refugees themselves; these are woven into the main narrative. Along the way I make some digressions, explaining a few of the less well-known facets of life in Africa, in Kenya, in Nairobi: the customs, the history, the language, the culture, the religious beliefs. I'll try to be a sort of tour guide through an unfamiliar territory. But I'll let the refugees speak for themselves, and when they speak I'll use their own words and cadences, sometimes in their own languages. All of these stories, of course, are now gathered from what Willa Cather called the "incommunicable past," but the sights, the sounds, and the voices are all emblazoned into my memory. I remember them quite well.

This is, then, a sort of spiritual journey, as well as a travel diary and a record of observations of humanity and human nature. It is also very much the story of a "missionary"—a word that before my time in Africa I disliked intensely. A word that conjured up images of the Great White Father dispensing God, as a sort of prize, to docile, uneducated natives.

In the end, though, I came away with a new understanding and appreciation of the word. "Mission," after all, comes from the Latin *missio*, meaning "to send." A missionary is simply one who is sent, and while in the past a missionary may have believed he or she was sent to *bring* God, I knew, like most of the people with whom I worked in East Africa, that my mission was more complex: to *find* God among the people—and to learn who God is for them.

And that particular mission I was able to accomplish, thanks to the refugees.

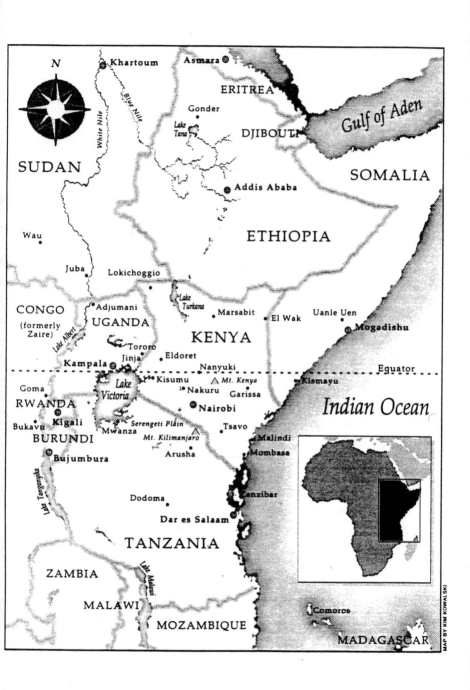

FINDING SISTER LUISE

Already in the few days I had spent in Nairobi, I found myself falling in love with Kenya. There is a quality about it which I have found nowhere else but in Ireland, a warm loveliness of breadth and generosity. It was not a matter of mere liking, as one likes any place where people are amusing and friendly and the climate is agreeable, but a feeling of personal tenderness.

—Evelyn Waugh, *Remote People*

The journey, of course, was very long. Twenty-seven sandy-eyed hours of flying, hopping from Boston to New York to Amsterdam to Nairobi. Thirteen of these hours, the last leg of the trip, were spent in a KLM jet, alternating my time between reading an exceedingly long biography of Harry Truman, watching three dull movies with Dutch subtitles, and staring intermittently at a tiny TV screen mounted over the heads of the passengers. The screen displayed a computerized chart that mapped our airborne progress over enormous chunks of land: Europe (are those the Alps?), the Mediterranean (is that Greece down there?), and northern Africa (yes, that is *definitely* the Sahara). At times the little plane on the screen appeared to be going backwards, so ponderous did the trip seem. For much of the flight I turned the same question over and over in my mind, like a disturbing mantra: what the hell am I doing?

Zombie-like, I finally stumbled onto the tarmac at Jomo Kenyatta Airport in Nairobi and found my way to Kenyan customs. After waiting one hour in line, I was confronted by an enormously fat Kenyan man who sat placidly behind an immense wooden desk, perched on a three-foot-high dais. He was illuminated by a single dim light bulb that hung suspended by a greasy black cord. Next to the desk stood a thinner man wearing a khaki uniform and a soft red beret.

"*Karatasi*," said the man in khaki. I assumed that this meant papers, and handed over my passport, vaccination booklet, and airline ticket. These he handed up to his boss behind the desk, who examined my ticket and shook his head dolefully.

"*Bwana*, this is not a return ticket," said the man behind the desk. "Give me your return ticket." He had a wonderful accent. *Re-tuhn*, he had said.

The man in the beret snapped his fingers at me. "Re-tuhn ticket." He snapped them again. Loudly this time.

"Return ticket?" I asked dumbly. "I have no return ticket. I'm coming here to *live*." I hoped that this show of solidarity with his country would impress the official. You have come to work with our *people*, he would say gratefully.

"If you do not have a re-tuhn ticket, you cannot be staying," he said instead.

Feeling fear—a new emotion following the cloudy boredom of the plane—I labored to explain my situation. I wasn't a tourist. I was going to be living here. For two years. As a missionary. With the Catholic church! I heard my voice jump an octave as I squeaked out the last piece of information.

"Besides," I added in a somewhat lower voice. "I have a *visa*."

He glanced at my passport. "This visa is no good here."

"But I got it at the Kenyan embassy!" I was squeaking again, and I heard the people behind me in line grunt their disapproval at this further delay in reaching their safari lodges.

"*Bwana*," he said evenly, "If you have no re-tuhn ticket, you *cannot* be entering this country." He turned to his assistant and handed him my papers. "Put him back on the plane."

I felt my face flush as I contemplated either a minor international incident or a twenty-seven-hour trip back to Boston. And given the fact that I had exactly fifty dollars on my person, the former was the more likely probability.

Then I remembered a strange document I carried in my pocket. A few weeks earlier, the Jesuit superior in Nairobi had sent me an inexplicable missive on letterhead stationery that read, in full: "Mr. James Martin, S.J., is a Jesuit and is known to us here at the Jesuit residence in Nairobi." At the bottom of the letter was a lurid red stamp that bore the legend: "Society of Jesus of East Africa." Accompanying this seemingly useless piece of paper was a cryptic note instructing me to hang on to the document "should there be any problems."

Though I had already told the man behind the desk every piece of information contained in the letter (and more) I was desperate. So, as the uniformed man led me away, gripping me tightly by the arm, presumably to insert me back on the KLM plane for another twenty-seven-hour flight, I remembered my document. "Wait!" I blurted out. "I have this," and flourished it toward the man at the desk.

He waved me back. I handed him the paper. He glanced at it briefly. "Ah," he said without reading its contents. "This stamp is very good." He motioned to me for my passport and stamped it with a loud thud: "Nairobi. 28 July 1992." I was in.

Two American Jesuits met me in the waiting room: Mike Evans, the director of JRS Nairobi, and Jim Corrigan, the other young Jesuit with whom I would live. The smallish airport, unairconditioned, was packed with tourists and Kenyan taxi drivers who held up hand-lettered signs welcoming eager Europeans and Americans looking forward to their first safari. It was 2 A.M. I asked Mike if it were always this crowded.

The airlines, he explained, arranged their schedules to accommodate European—not Kenyan—timetables. As a result, most of the major flights in and out of Nairobi arrived and left during the dead of the African night.

We walked through the parking lot and over to Mike's little blue Datsun. Tall palm trees rustled in a fresh, cool breeze. By habit I walked over to the right-hand side. "You want to drive?" Jim laughed. I peered through the window and saw the steering wheel. Oh, right. British cars.

We stowed my luggage in the trunk (or "boot" in this case) and after negotiating a few roundabouts pulled out onto the Mombasa Road, a smooth highway which in the opposite direction led in a straight line to the Indian Ocean, but in our case pointed to Nairobi. The night was entirely black; the Mombasa Road untroubled by streetlights. Mike pointed out invisible landmarks in the darkness: the game reserve, the industrial area, the center of town, a local hospital.

After an hour we reached Loyola House, the main Jesuit community in Nairobi. At the sound of the car, a thin Maasai man wrapped in a woolen blanket opened the iron gate. He smiled and waved as we entered the compound. I took a brief look around at Loyola House: a large community for fifteen or so Jesuits, an airy living room, dining room, and small chapel, all of which opened onto a pleasant courtyard. I found my room and then, for the first time in more than a day, climbed into bed and collapsed.

ON MY FIRST FULL DAY in Nairobi, Mike introduced me to two of the people with whom I would work: Sister Luise Radlmeier, an elderly Dominican sister from Germany who ran an education program for refugee children in the city, and Father Eugene Birrer, a Swiss priest from a small religious order called the Bethlehem Fathers. Father Eugene, by dint of his extensive experience in relief work, ran one of the Nairobi offices of the United Nations High Commissioner for Refugees. Though this was, I thought, an odd job for a priest—essentially a UN official—Eugene was eminently qualified and almost preternaturally efficient. On behalf of the UN, he provided official papers to every refugee who made his or her way to Nairobi. He also ran the income-generating activities for JRS in Nairobi. My time was to be split between Eugene and Luise, though I would work out of Sister Luise's office, a two-story flat a few blocks away from the Jesuit community.

Sister Luise was a large, *gemütlich* woman, who wore thick glasses that were perpetually askew. Her practical, everyday habit consisted of a white blouse, a blue wrap-around skirt, and a short blue veil that framed her face. I enjoyed working with her enormously. Sister Luise was also rather a legend among the thousands of Sudanese refugees in Nairobi.

During the past few years the Sudanese government, based in the northern capital of Khartoum, had carried out a systematic policy of exterminating the Nuba people as part of its war against other ethnic groups in southern Sudan. The Islamist government, run according to strict Islamic law (*Shari'ah*), had been at war with the South, where Christianity and traditional religions predominated. In response to the persecution (which included not only shelling of the villages but also enslavement, torture, and crucifixion) the Sudanese People's Liberation Army had sprung up. Later, the SPLA splintered into two smaller groups that immediately began fighting each other, plunging the South into further misery. (A few years before I moved to Nairobi, three Jesuits living in southern Sudan and teaching at a diocesan seminary had been abducted by the SPLA and marched through hundreds of kilometers of savanna before their eventual release.)

As a result, thousands of Sudanese left Sudan for northern Uganda. Many continued on to the refugee camps along the northern Kenyan border. And, as both government forces and Southern rebels pressed young boys into military service, one well-known contingent of boys marched thousands of kilometers from southern Sudan to refuge in Kenya, their ranks slowly diminished by starvation, disease, and wild animals. Some of the surviving boys had eventually found their way to Nairobi; many were enrolled in Sister Luise's education program.

It was to these people, particularly the children, that Sister Luise ministered. With little help from anyone other than her sisters in Germany, Sister Luise also set up what could only be called a small town for dozens of Sudanese refugees near her house in Juja, a few kilometers north of Nairobi. For these reasons she was justifiably famous throughout southern Sudan. Describing his journey to Nairobi, a very young Sudanese boy once said to me, "When I left Sudan, Brother, I knew that I had to be finding Sister Luise."

"You must come to visit me in Juja," Luise announced one day in her office, over a lunch of lentils and rice. And so that afternoon we went, piling into her small white Toyota. She drove, appropriately enough, as if she were on the *Autobahn*.

In an hour we reached Juja. In the middle of the small dusty town stood her three-story apartment building, peopled entirely by Sudanese. Our car was quickly surrounded by laughing children, who poured out of the buildings shouting, "Sistah! Sistah!"

She led me through the flats, which surrounded a large, open, concrete courtyard. In one room sat three women hunched over their sewing machines. This was one of the small business projects sponsored by JRS. In another, a mother silently nursed a small child as three others slept naked on a soiled mattress. She smiled and waved when she saw Luise. "Sistah!" Across the hall, three young Sudanese boys, wearing torn T-shirts and white jockey shorts, sat with their heads bowed over large sheets of paper that Sister Luise had given them that morning. With stubby crayons they were drawing their memories of Sudan: soldiers, guns, refugees, and people lying dead on the ground, blood flowing from holes in their heads. In the courtyard, women nursed babies, hung laundry, and cooked meals in dented tin pots over smoky charcoal fires.

"Look at all these people, Brother," Sister Luise said, wiping perspiration from her forehead. "How did they ever *find* me?"

Sister Luise's office in Nairobi, where I was assigned to work two days a week, provided school fees for hundreds of refugee children in the city. But it turned out that there was little work there since the generous Sister Luise employed, perhaps not surprisingly, five or six Sudanese refugees to help her. "We are very happy to have you here, Brother," she admitted, "but there is not much for you to do." As a result I spent more and more time at the UN office, helping Father Eugene with the income-generating projects.

While the education program in Nairobi was housed in a small flat, the UN office was a much larger operation—a compound of three houses secluded behind a high stockade fence. It was also difficult to miss. Dozens of refugees stood daily in a line that snaked through the neighborhood, peopled at the time mostly by Somalis: the women veiled in brightly colored silk cloths; the men wearing dirty white shirts and faded plaid *kikoi*, the traditional cloth worn wrapped around the waist.

Father Eugene cleared his cluttered desk one morning and explained to me the basics of the program he had recently started. It was quite simple: many of the refugees in Nairobi, while very poor, had marketable skills that they had learned in their home countries. In order to help them support themselves, JRS provided individuals and groups with grants (averaging around $1,000 per person—a princely sum in Kenya) to start their own businesses.

Finding interested refugees was never a problem; at the time, the UN estimated there were three million in Kenya.

KENYA LIES IN THE CENTER of a number of East African countries which, since the mid-1960s, have seen a staggering amount of violence. Its relatively stable environment has made it a magnet for refugees. The Rwandese began arriving in the 1960s, during an outburst of Tutsi–Hutu violence in Rwanda; the flow continued sporadically and exploded in mid-1994 after the genocide began. Typically, the Rwandese passed through Tanzania or Uganda on their journey to Kenya. In the late 1970s and early 1980s, as a result of the oppressive policies of Idi Amin

Dada and Milton Obote, Ugandans had also fled into neighboring Kenya, settling in the refugee camps in the arid Northwest.

Sister Luise's southern Sudanese friends began their exodus only a few years before my arrival. Thousands of Ethiopians had arrived during the regime of Haile Mariam Mengistu, the Socialist dictator who had deposed and executed Emperor Haile Selassie in 1974. More recently, the toppling of Mohammed Siad Barre's regime had provoked vicious clan warfare and country-wide starvation in Somalia, forcing hundreds of thousands of Somalis into northeastern Kenya.

Refugees remain in the squalid, overcrowded camps that line the Kenyan border for months, sometimes years. Often the UN repatriates refugees to their home countries. Occasionally refugees are resettled in the Kenyan countryside. And sometimes, because of medical needs or the desire to be reunited with family, they receive permission to move to Nairobi. Or, as was more often the case, they escape from the camps, fleeing the wretched life there, and make their own way to the city.

The UN estimated at the time that there were anywhere from 50,000 to 100,000 refugees living in Nairobi alone. Nearly all lived in extreme poverty. The majority of them knew about JRS, and many were desperate for a chance to start their own businesses.

As a result, Father Eugene was able to set up twenty projects in just a few short months: tailoring shops, carpentry shops, hair-dressing shops, a chicken farm, a printing press, a small restaurant, a bakery. An energetic Austrian friend of his, named Uta Fager, helped.

Uta had lived in Nairobi for a number of years with her husband Jürgen, a civil engineer. She had extensive experience in small business development, having worked, among other places, in India and Southeast Asia. Uta and Jürgen had filled their elegant Nairobi home with handicrafts and works of art from friends whom she had helped all over the world. More important, Uta took a genuine interest in the refugees' lives and in their personal situations. She was exceedingly generous and often dipped into her own funds to help the refugees through tough times: paying for house rent, clothes for a new baby, a funeral. I learned a great deal from the way Uta entered into their lives without being too bossy or controlling.

Because of his considerable UN responsibilities, Eugene spent most of his time in the office dealing with an unending stream of refugees looking for documentation. So while Eugene supervised the financial aspects of the small projects from his office, Uta met with the refugees and visited the businesses in the "field," that is, the slums of Nairobi.

I was assigned to work primarily with Uta, whom the refugees invariably called "Mrs. Uta." Names and forms of address were terribly important in East Africa. When the Kenyans and refugees referred to me first as "Father Jim," I protested. "I'm not ordained yet," I explained. "You can just call me Jim."

But this would never do for the refugees. "Jim" was simply too familiar, though when I started to call refugees by *their* last names ("Mr. Mujambere," "Mrs. Nabwire") I was swiftly instructed to call them by their first. It was simply a matter of respect for a religious personage. No matter how much I proclaimed my basic equality with the refugees, I remained for better or worse a figure of authority. When I met Sarah Nakate, a Ugandan refugee, I was astonished to watch her first curtsy and then kneel before me on a cold cement floor, a sign of respect in Uganda. It shocked my egalitarian American sensibilities. When I asked if she'd feel more comfortable sitting in a chair, the expression on her face told me that the answer was a decided no. Protesting was useless; eventually I accepted it for what it was— a sign of respect.

I was even more uncomfortable when shown such signs of respect by older refugees. One's age, I quickly learned, is a matter of no small importance in East Africa. In some villages, for example, children born during the same year are raised together in a closely knit group, their age binding them as near as siblings. More than once would a refugee, after discovering I was thirty-two years old, call me his "age-mate."

Moreover, advanced age is a badge of immense dignity in Kenya. The term *mzee* (pronounced "m-zay"), which is simply the Swahili word for "old," is a term of great honor. The common salutation "*Jambo, Mzee!*" is in Kenya the most respectful expression one can use. (The contrast to Western culture is strikingly evident when one imagines the response engendered by hailing someone with a hearty "Hello, Old Person!") When Marie Bugwiza, a young Rwandese refugee, introduced me one day to her mother, a grey-haired woman of nearly eighty, Marie treated her with exquisite dignity and care. Whenever her mother began to speak, Marie fell silent and turned toward her mother to listen attentively. Her actions reminded me to treat her mother and her mother's age-mates with the same good manners.

In response to some of these traditions I tried to learn how best to show respect in their cultures. Among many of the refugees, for example, greetings were central to demonstrating friendship. With good friends one embraced and kissed both cheeks: left, then right. (With very close friends, three kisses were called for: left, right, left.) To shake hands with an Ethiopian man or woman, one learned to cup one's own right elbow with the left hand, and bow. In fact, one shook hands with everyone in East Africa. Upon entering a room it was customary to make the rounds shaking each person's hand. It was considered shockingly rude to skip anyone. This custom became so ingrained that when I finally returned to the States, I was oddly embarrassed when I realized that I couldn't remember exactly what Americans did when entering a roomful of people.

I also learned a few greetings in the refugees' mother tongues: in Kinyarwanda for the Rwandese, Amharic for the Ethiopians, Luganda for the Ugandans, Arabic for some of the Sudanese, and Swahili for the rest. It was a simple and surprisingly effective way of putting at ease people whose cultures were either denigrated or ignored.

As for nomenclature, as Uta grudgingly answered to "Mrs. Uta" (though "*Frau* Uta" would have been more accurate), the refugees and I eventually settled on "Brother Jim." Technically, in Catholic religious parlance I was a "scholastic," not a religious brother, but it was pleasantly informal. I was happy not to be called "Father," and they were happy they could give me a type of honorific. And I liked the idea of being a brother to the refugees. But for a syntactical reason I never fully understood, both the refugees and local Kenyans used the title in almost every sentence when speaking with me: "I am sick today, Brother Jim." "You must be giving me some money, Brother Jim." "Yes, Brother." "No, Brother."

Once a refugee handed me a formal letter addressed to "Father Brother Jim." I asked her about the salutation.

She looked at me quizzically. "Well, you are a Father," she explained, "and your name is Brother Jim." Next question?

During my first few weeks in Nairobi, I took Swahili lessons at a small language school housed in a tiny flat. For a minimal fee paid by my Jesuit community, the Kiongozi Language School provided one-on-one tutoring for five hours in the afternoon. Our classroom was a cramped room with a single window high on the cinderblock wall. A small board painted black served as the blackboard, though there was rarely any chalk.

Geoffrey, a wiry Kenyan man with an affable disposition, was my teacher.

At one o'clock in the afternoon I walked through the broad fields behind Ngong Road to school. This is the time of day when many Kenyans take their *pumzika*, or nap. On the grass fields by the dirt path that led to the school were dozens of people enjoying their *pumzika*. Lying there on the dry brown grass, their faces toward the hot sun, they looked as if they had fallen from the sky. Geoffrey entered the classroom each day with dry grass stuck to his short hair.

Besides Swahili, Geoffrey also taught me a little *Sheng*, the lively patois favored by Nairobi teenagers. I also learned from him the basics of what might be called East African English: its vocabulary, its turns of phrase, its sometimes convoluted grammar. "Even now" and "somehow," for example, started off at least half of the sentences I heard. "And now ..." was often used at the beginning of a sentence, particularly one that summed up a plaintive tale. "And now, Brother, you see that I am crying to you for some money!"

The present continuous tense was used in preference to the present or past, lending a unique feel to conversations. In East Africa things didn't happen, or hadn't happened; they were always *happening*. I never discovered if this particular syntax came from the Swahili, Bantu, or colonial influence, but I noticed that the refugees used it almost exclusively. "And now Brother, I am needing a new sewing machine." "I knew I had to be finding Sister Luise."

The confluence of some of these linguistic traits could often prove confusing. One woman described the size of her family thusly: "Even now Brother I am having three babies!"

My very first language lesson proved to be an unexpected source of mirth for some of my Kenyan neighbors. Geoffrey's teaching method was more or less total immersion; he addressed me in Swahili for the entire four hours. On the first day, as I waited in the small classroom, I heard a knock on the door.

"*Hodi?*" said Geoffrey as he stuck his head through the doorway, smiling.

I sat mute and uncomprehending in my chair.

"*Hodi?*" he said again hopefully. This time he provided an answer. Motioning toward me with his hand, he said, "*Karibu!*"

Ah, I thought, clearly this means "How are you?" and "I am fine." We spent another minute or so repeating this little drama and refining my pronunciation. What I hadn't realized, however, was that the two words are used in East Africa solely to ask if one may enter a room or a house. *Hodi* is a sort of all-purpose "May I enter?" and *karibu,* the rather more common "Welcome."

After class ended I decided I would put my new-found Swahili to use. I already knew that greeting people on the street was the order of the day, and so when I wandered through the paths behind Ngong Road I addressed passers-by with a lusty "*Hodi?*" This provoked a combination of embarrassed stares, confused but polite smiles, and outright laughter, as they contemplated my request to open an unseen door. Upon returning to the Jesuit community I walked in the door, strode up to Domatila, our Kenyan receptionist, and proudly asked, "*Hodi?*"

Domatila burst out laughing. "Brother, you are already inside!"

But despite this initial misunderstanding, Geoffrey was an excellent teacher, and in a few weeks I felt comfortable enough to carry on basic conversations in Swahili. By the end of four months, I had even mastered a little Kenyan slang. I figured I was ready for full-time work.

THE ROAD TO
AND FROM THIKA

And now faith, hope and love abide, these three;
and the greatest of these is love.

—*1 Corinthians 13:13*

"You really should visit a camp," said Uta one day over lunch at the UN office. "You can learn a lot from talking with the refugees here," she explained, "but you need to see where they have come from." There was, she told me, a camp near Juja, where Sister Luise lived. It was in the town called Thika, about thirty minutes north of Nairobi, and Sister Luise could certainly get me in. "She knows everyone in that town."

A few days later Sister Luise and I drove to Juja together. She was to drop me off at the camp, and in the evening I would take a *matatu*, a minibus, back to Nairobi. The Kenyan policeman at the gate, holding a semi-automatic rifle in his hand, swung open the gate as soon as he saw Luise's car. She chatted amiably with him in her thickly accented English, established my credentials, wished me luck, waved, and sped off, leaving clouds of red dust in her wake.

ONLY A FEW KILOMETERS AWAY from Nairobi, the Thika Reception Centre is at an unusual location for a Kenyan camp; most are situated along the borders—closer to the influx of the thousands of refugees who pour into Kenya. In Nairobi before my visit I had interviewed a Somali man named Ali, who had stayed in the camp. His story, which I recorded on tape, helped me better to understand the plight of the refugees in Thika.

My name is Ali. I am fifty-three years old. My father was a tailor in a hospital in Somalia for thirty years, and he died in 1974. My mother died when I was very young. My family lived in Mogadishu. Mogadishu is now destroyed, but before the dictatorship of Siad Barre, it was a small city where people lived in peace. At the age of seventeen, I left Mogadishu to study in Italy—this was before the independence of Somalia. I studied in Florence, a city I liked very much. I have many good impressions of Florence, a city full of culture and very beautiful. In the University of Florence, I was studying for my doctorate in philosophy. After I finished my oral examination in Florence, I went for two years study in Germany.

Thika was designed as a temporary holding camp for roughly three hundred to five hundred refugees, but during the week of my visit it held more than five thousand people—mostly Somalis, Ugandans, Ethiopians, and Sudanese. Many had been there for three or four years, awaiting repatriation to their home countries or to places like the United States or Canada. The camp itself resembled many of the slums scattered throughout Nairobi, slums I would later come to know well: wood-and-mud houses, ears of corn roasting over small charcoal fires, open sewers, and trash everywhere. There was a severe lack of toilet facilities (enough to accommodate only the original five hundred people) and a resulting foul smell around the camp.

I was surprised to see a few shops and kiosks selling sodas and other small items. There was even a shop tucked under a tin roof in the middle of the camp that sold small chairs and stools. But unlike the slums in Nairobi, the Thika camp is bordered by barbed wire and patrolled by Kenyan police officers.

> *After I graduated, I returned to Mogadishu, where I taught at the university, which is very small. First I was teaching full-time, and then part-time. For about twenty-five years I was teaching philosophy of law. For many years, I waited to get married, because my father had two wives and each one had five children. I waited such a long time because I had to earn money for my brothers and sisters. In 1981, I married my wife Asha, and I have six children. The first baby died when he was small, only two years old.*

The houses in Thika were simple. Some refugees brought a small amount of money with them and were able to purchase wood for small shelters. Most, however, lived in plain mud houses held together by branches.

Malnutrition was an enormous problem, particularly among the children. Because of the large pools of stagnant water in the camp, malaria was also common. Rice was served twice a day, and meat, according the refugees with whom I spoke, was a rarity. "Look at what we get to eat here," said a young Ethiopian man approaching me. He held out a large bowl of rice. I asked him how many times a day he ate.

"Twice a day, Brother."

"Is that enough for you?"

"It is not. This is all we get. Just rice and maybe some corn. I am always hungry. And he is hungry, too," he said, and pointed to his son.

> *I was living in peace in Mogadishu with my family. But there were many tribal problems in the country, and my*

tribe is in the minority. I stayed in Mogadishu until December 1991.

The war was tragedy, tragedy. The atrocities were very, very prevalent, with people dying in the streets. There were many tanks and the soldiers all had machine guns. They were using mortars. The situation was bad—very dangerous.

In the entire camp there was only one social worker to cope with an enormous caseload of thousands of people, all with severe problems—hunger, sickness, family worries, resettlement concerns, and fear. She found it difficult to deal with the endless strain of cases and the fact that every refugee she saw wanted the same thing. "They all want more food," she explained to me sadly. "But I have to tell them, if I give their child more food, I have to do the same with everyone else. What else can I do?"

Apart from waiting for food, there was very little to do at Thika. Occasionally, there might be a soccer ball for children to use on a large, barren field, but it was a precious commodity. Most of the men and women there, as in other refugee camps, spent a good deal of time squatting in the doorways of their small homes, waiting. The overall effect of the camp—the poverty, the smell, the halted lives of the refugees—evoked a wave of sadness that passed over me like a physical thing.

During the night of December 11, 1991, we left Mogadishu with the help of a gunman I had paid money to. I left with my wife and four children. My wife was pregnant—five months along. We were all frightened. Fortunately, we had strength. And it was life or death. It was impossible to stay in Mogadishu. Every day one hundred or two hundred people would be killed.

An array of East Africans surrounded me in the camp: darker-skinned Sudanese women carrying clay water jugs on their heads; bearded Ethiopian men talking in the sun outside the small Ethiopian church in the camp; young, olive-skinned

Somali boys with long plaid *kikoi* wrapped around their waists, walking hand in hand; Somali women wearing vividly colored, patterned fabrics. Surprisingly, however, there were few fights, even with so many ethnic groups living together. I asked one Ethiopian man why he thought there was little violence. "Here we must all survive together," he said, "so we cannot fight."

The children, in particular, mixed freely, speaking English, Swahili, Luganda, Amharic, Acholi, Kinyarwanda, and Arabic, seemingly unconcerned with any differences separating them. And most of them appeared to be very much at home in the camp. Indeed, one refugee told me that many boys and girls, in the past few years in the camp, had grown into adulthood.

> *First we went to Uanle Uen, a town ninety kilometers from Mogadishu. It is a small farming town, and I thought it would be very quiet. But after four months, the soldiers of Siad Barre came, and there was new aggression. So my family and I escaped from Uanle Uen to Kenya, on foot.*
>
> *All my things, all my family . . . for twenty-nine days we walked. After five hours of walking, we would stop to prepare a little food and water for the children. There were nomads who would bring us water. We were all worried, the children especially. We would sleep on the ground. For twenty-nine days. And much of the time we were very sick.*
>
> *On May 8, 1992, my wife was delivered of a child in the hospital at the refugee camp at El Wak, in Kenya, with no complications and without problems, thanks to the goodness of the people and the local authorities who helped us.*

My visit provoked a great deal of curiosity, and many of the refugees were interested in talking. I was stopped a number of times by people running up to ask questions. "Have you come from America?" "Can I call you if I get to Nairobi?" "Do you have any money, Brother?" "Will you take me back to Nairobi with you?"

One young Ethiopian boy greeted me and asked me who I was and why I had come to Thika. I told him that I was a Jesuit working with refugees. "Oh," he said smiling, "you know that the gifts of the Holy Spirit are faith, hope, and love, and the greatest of these is love." And then he ran off into the maze of shacks surrounding us, leaving me wondering what had prompted his unexpected comment.

Finally, we were able to get some UN protection letters and we arrived in Nairobi, after we had stayed in the Thika camp. But now I have nothing. I haven't any money. I haven't any job. My family is worried, worried.

And in Nairobi, the police never leave us alone. One day, they wanted to take me away—to one of the refugee camps. But I told them, "I cannot go. I am ill." Finally, I had to give each of them fifty shillings and they released me.

My family is always closed up in the house. But the police know where we are. They don't come in the house, but they wait in the streets. When they see you in the street they catch you—like fish. I have five children, all small. My health is not good. I want to go somewhere else now because my family is very, very worried—very afflicted. We just want peace now.

As I was leaving the camp to catch the *matatu*, a small Sudanese boy wearing an oversized T-shirt and faded blue shorts approached me. He had fashioned a toy out of a straightened wire hanger that he connected to a pair of tiny wheels from a toy car. He pushed the wheels in endless circles in the dirt. He looked up and said softly in Swahili, "*Unaenda wapi?*" Where are you going?

I told him I was returning to Nairobi.

"Oh," he said, staring at the ground. "*Ninakaa hapa.*" I'm staying here.

Don Doll SJ

The poor in Nairobi took care not to waste things. Here, a child in one of the slums plays with a "car" he has fashioned from old wires, sticks, dead batteries, tin cans, and twigs.

TAKATAKA

One survival technique is a lack of wastefulness;
the African puts everything to use.

—David Lamb, *The Africans*

Kenyans burn all their trash outdoors. During my first month of work, I asked Sister Luise when the trash collectors came to our neighborhood. She just laughed, "Brother, *we* are the trash collectors!"

Near every Kenyan house or flat or set of flats—from the president's residence to the simplest shack in the poorest slum—there is a trash pile. Houses in tonier neighborhoods wall off their trash piles with tall wooden fences; in the slums there is typically one large dump for everyone, which is constantly smoldering. As a result, there is always and everywhere in the city the pungent smell of burning garbage. Often, to start the fire, eucalyptus leaves will be added, which perfumes the city air with an improbably sweet incense. This—combined with the diesel fumes belching out of ancient trucks, the red clay wet by the rain, and the aroma of roasting ears of corn sold on the street corners—is the scent of Nairobi.

Behind the JRS office was hidden our own trash dump, fed mostly by garbage, eucalyptus leaves, old folders, letters, and miscellaneous paper products. During "tea breaks," at ten and four o'clock, our staff consumed a mixture of sweet milk and tea cooked in a large, dented tin pot. Tea was always accompanied by thick slices of white bread slathered with "Blue Band," a greasy, local margarine product. Blue Band came in a bright yellow can encircled by, not surprisingly, a bright blue band. So along with the burnt garbage and leaves, charred Blue Band tins piled up higher and higher in the dump.

You had to be careful what you threw out. Much of what we considered waste was not always considered *takataka*, or trash, by the Kenyans and the refugees. Used envelopes and folders that I had tossed onto our trash pile were cleaned and neatly smoothed down; I would later spy them on someone's desk. After I threw out some old magazines, one of the Kenyan women who worked with us at the JRS office ran outside, walked into the fire, and carefully plucked them out of the conflagration. I noticed her slip them into her jacket and made a mental note to ask her if she'd like to read my magazines after I had finished with them. There was, I found, something inexpressibly sad about my trash being sought after by the friends with whom I worked.

At the Jesuit community one day, I tossed out a copy of a Jesuit newsletter in the house dump, along with old letters and some month-old newspapers that had been brought by a visiting American. I lit the fire with eucalyptus leaves and the wooden kitchen matches that lay under a wooden plank. As I walked away from the fire I noticed our *askari*, our watchman, a Maasai man named Joseph, picking through the smoking garbage.

Not long afterwards, as I was chatting with Joseph in his guard shack by the front gate, I noticed that he had tacked up some pictures from the *Time* magazine I had tossed away, their edges curled black from the fire: a picture of Bill Clinton, and an advertisement for perfume—Ralph Lauren for Men. Next to these was posted a photo clipped from our Jesuit province newsletter: a gathering of a dozen men on the steps of a local

Jesuit high school. Joseph caught me staring at the picture. I told him that I knew those people who were pinned on his wall.

"I am so happy," he said, "to be having your friends in my house, Brother."

A Chicken Farm, the 241N Machine, and a Visit to Safi Textiles

The joy and hope, the grief and anguish, of the people of our time, especially of those who are poor or afflicted in any way, are the joy and hope, the grief and anguish of the followers of Christ.
—*Gaudium et Spes,* "The Pastoral Constitution on the Church in the Modern World," The Second Vatican Council

In order to receive a business grant from JRS, a refugee was asked to complete a lengthy process that included filling out a number of forms (illiterate refugees often paid friends for this task) and visiting our office for two or three interviews. The refugees also had to demonstrate some expertise in the business they were planning to run. A woman might be asked, for example, to bring in a sample of her sewing or a certificate from a sewing course. At some point before the awarding of a grant, Uta and I visited the refugee's home. After the grant was awarded, we would monitor the project, offering advice and generally helping to smooth the bumpy roads that the refugees faced.

We made it clear to the refugees that these businesses were most emphatically *their* businesses though the initial seed money came from us. They were not our employees; they had complete freedom to make decisions. We felt this particular emphasis was important in order to afford them the dignity and satisfaction that came with running their own businesses.

SINCE UTA HAD ALREADY worked with the refugees for more than a year, she had acquired an encyclopedic knowledge of the different business groups, the slums where they lived, and their various products. I was impressed with her acumen and her good-natured relationship with the refugees; I hoped that I would someday be as trusted as she was.

When I arrived, Uta and Eugene were already mentoring twenty or so separate projects. The diversity was astonishing.

We sponsored, for example, a chicken farm located in a slum called Riruta, quite near our office. Uta had decided that I should begin visiting the refugees in the field as soon as possible. And since the chicken farm was running into difficulties, Uta thought it was the perfect time to pay them a visit.

We must have made an improbable pair. Uta was a strikingly elegant woman who wore bangles and bracelets from her days in India, necklaces made by the refugees in Kenya, and, more often than not, blouses and skirts made of light, flowing fabrics. As for me, it took a while to figure out what would be appropriate to wear. A clerical collar was out of the question—way too hot. Jeans were too warm as well. In the end, I found khaki pants and a short-sleeved cotton shirt about right. Old sneakers were fine, too, since any shoes I wore would invariably become caked with Nairobi's adhesive mud. A backpack was handy for carrying a sweater—in case it suddenly got chilly—and pens and papers for any notes. Doubtless, though, the two of us were quite recognizable as we stepped through mud and garbage on the way to the refugees' homes in the slums.

"Halloo!" Uta shouted cheerfully as she entered someone's house or business, in this case a low wooden shack with hundreds of peeping chicks running crazily on the dirt floor. The chicken farms (in time we would eventually sponsor three) were a perpetual headache for the refugees who ran them. Chickens, I was told by the refugees who raised them, are extremely prone to disease, particularly in East Africa. They were constantly dying, resulting in the eruption of bitter battles between the refugees and the hatcheries that provided the chicks. "Ha!" said Samuel Mujambere, a Ugandan refugee, as I stood hunched over in his dark chicken coop, "Look at these chicks, Brother! Surely you can be seeing that they are *very* sick!"

Given my limited experience with chicken illnesses, I admitted I certainly could *not* see they were sick, but that I took his word for it nevertheless. Sure enough, a few days later Samuel entered my office bearing a dead yellow chick in his hand (he carried it to my office on the *matatu*, he said) for me to inspect. "They are all dead, Brother," he said sadly. Then followed three weeks of angry telephone calls (Samuel and I alternated calls) to the Nakuru Hatcheries demanding a refund, which he eventually received.

The next batch of chicks fared much better, and a few months later, instead of bringing me a dead chick, Samuel walked into my office smiling. He opened his fist to reveal a single brown egg. "*Tumepona!*" he said triumphantly. "We have recovered!"

We also sponsored a small bakery, where the eight Rwandese women who worked together seemed to be forever quarreling. They christened their business the Engabire Bakery, after the Kinyarwandese word for "gift." They baked tasty loaves of white and brown bread, which were, unfortunately, exactly one shilling more expensive than the normal priced breads in the market.

This made marketing the loaves a challenge. Our other projects included two Ethiopian restaurants; a carpentry shop run by three Ugandan refugees; two *dukas*, or general stores; a dairy farm; a Rwandese woman named Césaire who made beaded necklaces; two women who made batiks and tie-dye fabrics; two hairdressing "saloons" (not "salons," I was told, "saloons"); and a Ugandan man named Joseph who made metal crutches and prosthetic legs, which he sold to Somali war victims.

Our tailoring projects (which varied in size from one woman with her machine at home to ten women working in a cooperative) were by far the most numerous of the small businesses. It seemed that all of the women refugees—Rwandese, Ethiopian, Ugandan, Sudanese—knew how to sew and, for purposes of our application process, it was easy to verify that they did. Tailoring projects were also simple to set up. We only needed to provide a machine, some thread, and some fabric. We ended up purchasing so many sewing machines for the refugees—fifteen in my first year alone—that I eventually struck up a deal with Amedo Sewing, a tiny Singer sewing machine outlet on Koinange Street in Nairobi. "Brother, you are our very best customer," they said wonderingly whenever I called to order two or three more machines.

Over time I would become quite expert at selecting the right machines for the tailoring projects. At the outset, and before I knew any better, I purchased the most expensive machines (on the theory that the expensive machines would be the most useful) only to find out later that many of the women hadn't the faintest idea how to use them. From then on, I stuck with the simpler, sturdier machines; they were easy to use and less likely to need repairs. The Singer 241N (with straight-line sewing, button-making capacity, and a zigzag feature) was our machine of choice.

As for the material, we provided the women with checks to present to the fabric shops in town. This, however, gave rise to a problem.

Most of the fabric stores in Nairobi are run by people the

Kenyans call, somewhat derisively, "Asians." Shiva Naipaul wrote, in his insightful book *North of South*:

> *I dislike the term: it was coined as a convenient shorthand to lump together all of the peoples of the subcontinent. However, since it is so firmly established in current usage, I shall not cavil. It has, in any case, acquired its own emotional charge. I accept it as a peculiarly East African political category—not as a universal badge of "identity."*

These Indians and Pakistanis, descendants of families who had emigrated with the British during the colonial expansion (or whose forced passage attended the building of the East African Railway), provide a critical merchant class to countries in the region. But because of their status, they are often disliked by other locals. Idi Amin, for example, kicked out all "Asians" and other non-Ugandans from his country in 1972, satisfying the prejudicial wish of Ugandans to wrest control of all businesses from non-Ugandan hands. Unfortunately for all concerned, Amin's ill-advised decision merely brought the country to an economic standstill, at least as far as small businesses were concerned, a situation from which it is still recovering. More recently, the "Asians" have been invited back by the current Ugandan government.

In Kenya, though, there had been no such action from a government that, despite other shortcomings, seemed to understand the importance of the "Asian" merchant class. And so "Asian" businesses in downtown Nairobi, particularly in such commodities as cloth, thread, and small machines, flourished. This economic success, however, came at a price.

Jacqueline was a Ugandan refugee who had Hansen's disease, or leprosy. She had three fingers on her right hand, and two and a thumb on her left. Jacqueline spoke little English, so we communicated through a friend who translated her Luganda. She made small mice out of terrycloth and foam rubber, which she sold for ten shillings apiece to children in her neighborhood. But her physical condition made it terribly difficult to do the close work needed for sewing. So after a few interviews, Uta and I decided to provide her with a machine and some material.

The day her project was approved I wrote out a check for 500 shillings payable to the "Safi Textile Company," a fabric store in town. She beamed when I handed her the check and said something to her translator in Luganda.

"She says she will be making many, many mice with this check," said the translator.

A few hours later Jacqueline returned with her friend. She presented me with the folded check, uncashed. The translator related that the store had simply refused to cash the check. Perhaps they didn't recognize the name of our organization, I said, and wrote a cover letter for Jacqueline to bring with her the next time. I gave them money for the bus, and off they went. They were back again in a few hours, and after talking with the two I discovered that not only wouldn't the merchants cash her check, they had refused even to *speak* with them, check or no. I decided to accompany Jacqueline to Safi.

The next morning, the three of us piled into my jeep and drove into Nairobi. They directed me to Safi Textiles, located on Kijabe Road, a narrow thoroughfare running behind the Norfolk Hotel, crowded with seed distributors, tour companies, sign makers, and assorted other establishments. Safi itself is sandwiched between two much larger fabric merchants. I parked a discreet distance from the store. "Why don't you try again," I suggested. They looked at me, doubtful.

In a few minutes they emerged from the store. "He has kicked us out again, Brother!"

Angry and annoyed, I entered the shop with check in hand, while Jacqueline and her friend leaned on the jeep chatting under the hot sun. The gloomy interior of the shop consisted of rows and rows of dark wooden shelves holding huge bolts of colorful cloth, and a long glass counter, behind which a number of Kenyan employees stood placidly. Far in the back of the store, an enormous Indian fellow—the owner I supposed—sat on a tall stool. He leaped up and rushed to the counter.

"Yes, sir," he said. "May I be of some help?"

Rather than remonstrate with him, I decided it would be more effective simply to explain the situation. It was more urgent, I thought, to help the refugees than it was to vent my anger. The Jesuit Refugee Service was prepared to send all of the refugees here and provide Safi Textiles with a great deal of business. Was he interested in this? "Absolutely!" Could I have his word that he would treat the refugees with dignity? "Absolutely!"

Emerging into the bright sun, I called Jacqueline and her friend into the store. The owner smiled beatifically. In a few minutes Jacqueline purchased a few yards of pink terrycloth—at a discount, I noted.

This kind of prejudice wasn't confined to a few shopkeepers in town. More serious from the standpoint of the refugees were the prejudices they often experienced from local Kenyans. Quite naturally, poor Kenyans resented anyone who might pose a threat of taking jobs away from them. In northern Kenya, where the refugee camps had sprung up, word had gotten around that refugees enjoyed a better life than the locals, thanks to the UN (which provided them with housing) and sundry relief organizations (which provided them with almost everything else). This too caused considerable tension and occasional violence against the refugees in the camps.

When refugees living in Nairobi were perceived as doing "well," or at least better than the local Kenyans, they were sometimes subject to jealous reprisals. One woman, after we provided her with a large sewing machine (in retrospect, too large and too expensive) returned home one day and found her house burned to the ground. Another, whose landlord saw her little tailoring business flourishing, promptly raised her rent, destroying her meager profits.

Josée Mukagaga, a Rwandese woman trying to start a fish-and-chips shop with a friend, asked me on a number of occasions to visit her at home. One afternoon I offered to drive to her home in Dandora, a large slum on the other side of town. I figured that she would be happy at my coming and also at the prospect of saving the bus fare. But I saw immediately from the expression on her face that she was not. She lowered her head.

"I am sorry, Brother. You cannot be coming today," she told me. "My landlord is at home, and if she is seeing you visit, she will surely be raising my rent." She explained that when the landlords saw a white face, they also saw money. Not until her landlord was visiting relatives up country did I finally visit Josée.

Later I would learn that the landlord heard of my secret visit from a neighbor of Josée and raised her rent anyway.

STANDARD

Driving in Kenya can be a hair-raising endeav-
our.... Visiting drivers should follow the traffic
laws that they know, not the example of local
daredevils.

—*Fodor's Guide to Kenya & Tanzania*

One of my greatest fears before reaching
Nairobi was what, precisely, I would do about
driving. I had never before used a standard trans-
mission, and I knew I would have to learn to do so on the left-
hand side of the road.

Driving in Nairobi, even for the most talented stick-shifters,
was a difficult proposition. The city's main roads were generally
one narrow lane in each direction. As a result, one needed to veer
into the other lane if one wished to pass—dramatically increasing the chances of running headlong into another car, which
drivers often did. Pedestrians stepped into the roads at will,
seemingly unconcerned with such matters as automobile traffic.
In her book *The Ukimwi Road*, which documents her travels

from Kenya to Zimbabwe, Dervla Murphy provides this wonderful description of motoring in East Africa's largest city:

> *I hadn't planned to linger in Nairobi and Day One did not tempt me to change my mind. At dawn, psychopathic drivers were already racing each other up and down Cathedral Road. Negotiating the junction to cross Kenyatta Avenue brought me out in a cold sweat.*

The streets themselves were in wretched condition. The city's few asphalt roads were full of enormous axle-breaking potholes. ("Speed bumps are the smoothest part of the road," more than one resident would tell me.) And more often than not the asphalt roads would be only *half* asphalt—the rest would be dirt; where the asphalt met the dirt the car's wheels would discover a foot-long drop. For most of the year, the dusty, hardpacked dirt paths made for bumpy rides. Driving in a car on the undulating roads of Nairobi was akin to being on an unruly horse. As the car lurched up and down passengers gripped onto the dashboard, the seats, the roof for stability. Finally, during the rains the roads became impassable rivers of red silt.

Because of the lack of working streetlights in Nairobi, drivers made liberal use of high-beams during the night, blinding oncoming drivers. The omnipresent Nairobi minibuses, the *matatus* (after *mapesa matatu,* "three shillings"), drove crazily on the poor roads. *Matatu* drivers earned their income based on the number of passengers they could squeeze into their small vehicles, and they raced through the crowded city streets to overtake rival *matatus* at the next stop. I once saw a *matatu,* speeding through a tight turn, flip over and spill dozens of people out onto the street. After a few minutes of shaking their fists menacingly at the driver, the disgruntled passengers simply righted the *matatu,* which quickly sped off. Another standard sight was that of huge diesel trucks struggling up the steep hills of Nairobi, creating long, snaking lines of cars behind them, waiting to pass, ever anxious to speed into the oncoming lane of cars on the right.

Over time I became good friends with Alice Nabwire, a Ugandan refugee.
Alice was tremendously proud of her small tailoring business in the Ngando
section of Nairobi, which was called ALANA Tailoring, where she worked
with two other refugee women.

But poor roads were not simply a danger to travelers and pedestrians: the conditions of the roads, mirrored throughout the continent, prevented commerce from spreading as efficiently as it might have with a more developed infrastructure. As Tanzania's first president, Julius Nyerere, famously commented, while the great powers were trying to get to the moon, "In Africa we are still trying to get to the next village."

Finally, to remind citizens of the dangers of driving, Nairobi's largest newspaper, the *Daily Nation,* published (in a prominent box on page three) a daily, year-to-date tab of the number of people killed in road accidents in Kenya. Next to that figure was last year's total.

So it was with great trepidation that I began my lessons a few months after my arrival. One of the Jesuits in my community generously offered to teach me the ins and outs of standard transmissions. For the next two weeks I sat placidly in one of the Jesuit community's cars as he tooled around the neighborhood, lecturing me about the manifold, the carburetor, the gaskets. I learned how to change a tire. Eventually, I learned how to shift gears, drive on the left, and negotiate a Kenyan roundabout.

Soon I was driving on my own. JRS had purchased a fifteen-year-old, sand-colored Suzuki jeep for the equivalent of $1,000. I was happy to have it, as it would allow me to visit the refugees more easily. Sadly, only three out of four gears worked at one time, there were no shock absorbers to speak of, the back door flew open at will, and the engine made a terrific din. But it had the advantage of being able to go into almost any part of the country—Nairobi slum or Kenyan game reserve.

Long drives were a frequent diversion during those first few months, as I found myself with a considerable amount of free time on my hands. Jim Corrigan, the other young Jesuit assigned to JRS, had left a few days after my arrival for a four-month language program on the banks of Lake Victoria in Tanzania. Jim thought that he might be staying for a longer period of time in East Africa, and so the extra Swahili studies would be of use. I opted for the program in Nairobi primarily because I wanted a more "Kenyan" Swahili and also because I wasn't keen on studying at a place where its students were expected to fall ill with malaria at least once during their sojourn. With Jim away, I knew few people other than the refugees and the friendly but decidedly sexagenarian Jesuits in my community. On top of this, I missed my friends and family at home immensely. In short, I was lonely.

And so I decided it would be a fine time to explore the city with our new car. After work, I would climb into the jeep and attempt to find my way around Nairobi—through the busy streets in the center of town, choked with *matatus* and Land Rovers; into the sprawling slums that blanketed three-quarters of the Kenyan capital; and onto the shady streets of the few wealthy neighborhoods, where the houses of expats and white Kenyans lay hidden behind great mounds of white bougainvillea. Occasionally I would venture outside Nairobi, and the clogged city streets would open up into long tarmac roads that sliced across the broad savanna, affording the occasional glimpse of a zebra, giraffe, or gazelle.

The rusty jeep was not a distinctive looking car, but the refugees were soon able to recognize it bouncing down the street. When they saw me they requested rides, much as they would hail a *matatu*: right arm out, palm down, pumping up and down. When I left work in the evening I was rarely alone. One day, three refugees climbed into the tiny space behind the two front seats. They laughed as we bounced down a rutted dirt path. Over the rumbling engine they shouted, "We are just like chickens being taken to the market!" More laughter.

Curiously, neither the Kenyans nor the refugees ever seemed to want me to do any work on the car, particularly if it involved getting my clothes soiled. If I washed it, they protested, "Brother, you should not be doing that!" This, I imagined, was considered beneath my dignity as a "priest," or maybe below my station as a white man. Or perhaps they simply wanted to do it themselves, for a fee. One day, off of Waiyaki Way, a large highway in Nairobi, I got a flat tire, a "puncture." I pulled off the highway onto the dirt shoulder of the road and began to change the tire. As I was doing so, a *matatu* sidled up beside me, waiting to drive onto the main highway. Turning around, I noticed everyone peering down at me.

"Father, you must be letting *me* do that!" one man said out of the window. "I will do that!" he said over the noise of the engine.

I laughed and, over my shoulder, asked him if he thought a white person couldn't change a tire. Yes, he answered at once, that's exactly what he imagined. The other passengers laughed with him as the *matatu* pulled away.

White drivers also attracted the attention of the impoverished Kenyan police, who regularly flagged down motorists to demand bribes. Traffic laws were created on the spot—laws, of course, that you had broken. You had, for example, passed another car by driving in the opposite lane (which everyone did), you had exceeded the speed limit (which was not posted), you were going down a one-way street (also not posted). And now you needed to pay a fine, and you needed to do so immediately. That one was a priest or brother or sister often helped to dissuade the police from levying their fines. But not every time.

Pulling me over in broad daylight, a policeman once informed me that my headlights were out. Initially, I thought to apologize, but then, I wondered aloud how he could tell, as it was the middle of the day.

"I can tell," he said simply. "Five hundred shillings."

I switched on the headlights and emerged from the jeep.

Bending down, I peered into the headlights. "Look," I said pointing. "They're working." No, he said, they were not.

This went on for some time until I knelt in the dirt and cupped my hands around one of the headlights, attempting to convince him of his mistake. He finally tired of the debate and waved me away.

There were a number of proven ways to respond to greedy police officers. One Tanzanian Jesuit, when accosted by the Kenyan police, would announce that his car was the property of the Catholic archdiocese (technically it was not, but close enough). Would the officer like to get in the car and visit the cardinal to collect his fee? Nothing, though, worked as well as simply ignoring the police as they stood by the side of the road and flagged you down. Because the police had, in point of fact, no cars with which to chase offending drivers.

ALICE NABWIRE, a Ugandan refugee, and I were driving home from the office one afternoon. I liked Alice enormously; in time we would become close friends. She ran a small tailoring business called ALANA Tailoring where she employed two other Ugandan refugees, Mary and Joyce. Alice had a sunny disposition; she smiled and laughed constantly, and teased me about a great many things: my gullibility (she thought other refugees were likely to take advantage of me if I weren't vigilant), my poor Swahili accent, and my sorry little jeep. For me, Alice, who remained hopeful in the face of a difficult life, personified the quote from St. Paul: "We are afflicted in every way, but not crushed; perplexed but not driven to despair ... struck down, but not destroyed."

Alice was also among the savviest and most persistent of the refugees I knew. Early on I discovered that I could sell some of her dresses and shirts to friends in Nairobi. If I chose two of her dresses, however, she would ask me to buy three. If I asked her to make three dresses she would say how much cheaper it would be to make four. Usually I gave in.

After one such negotiation I agreed to drive Alice home to Ngando, a slum a few kilometers from our office. In the middle of her asking why I hadn't purchased more of her dresses, a policeman flagged us down by the side of the road. I dutifully pulled over. Alice sank in her seat as the car slowed down. The Kenyan police were notoriously cruel to refugees, harassing them, beating them, tearing up their United Nations ID cards.

"*Jambo sana*," I said cheerfully to the officer.

"License please," he said.

I passed the license to Alice who handed it to the police

officer. He stared grimly at Alice and then examined my license. I had forgotten that the Jesuit superior at our community suggested I obtain one that read: "Fr. James Martin."

"Oh, *pole sana.*" Sorry. He waved me on, and I started the car.

Alice was astonished. Clearly this was different from the treatment of a refugee at the hands of the police. It did not go unnoticed. "Surely, Brother," said Alice as we pulled back onto the highway, "it is wonderful to be white."

AFRICAN SCARVES

The poor are accepted as constituting the prima-
ry recipients of the Good News and, therefore, as
having an inherent capacity to understand it
"better" than anyone else.

—Jon Sobrino, SJ,
The True Church and the Poor

One persistent challenge that the refugee businesses faced, particularly the tailoring projects,
was finding customers. Three major problems
conspired to prevent the refugees from selling their goods. First,
the most obvious and accessible market, their neighbors in the
slums, were too poor to purchase their goods. Second, the booming tourist markets in Nairobi, another natural venue, required
quantities far in excess of what their small projects could provide.
Finally, those customers who could afford to buy the refugees'
wares—tourists, wealthy Kenyans, and expats—were reluctant to
wander around the slums of Nairobi in search of bargains.

So, early on, I figured it might be a good idea to tap into the
rather large market of priests and religious communities in town.

This was one area where I thought that I might be able to be of some practical assistance to Uta (and the refugees). Nairobi was the unofficial religious headquarters of East Africa, and most Catholic religious congregations had at least one house in town. The outlying suburb of Karen (named for Karen Blixen, who wrote *Out of Africa* under the name Isak Dinesen) was referred to as "Little Vatican" in honor of the large number of religious communities that made their homes there. And there were dozens of Catholic priests, brothers, and sisters who daily trooped through our office to visit Sister Luise and me. Many of them expressed their admiration for the refugee handicrafts that increasingly crowded our offices. Perhaps, I thought, I could ask the refugee sewing groups to make some liturgical stoles, the long strips of fabric worn by priests celebrating Mass. An African-style stole would probably be the best, I thought. More authentic. Certainly more marketable.

But I wasn't sure what an "African" style would be. A few weeks earlier I had made a first visit to the Jesuit school of theology in Nairobi, called Hekima College (from the Swahili word meaning "wisdom.") The school's chapel featured a magnificent mural behind the altar, so striking that it had been featured in a recent article on African art in *Time* magazine. Twenty feet long and ten feet high, the mural itself was surrounded by enormous red, orange, and yellow chevrons, whose colors radiated out in long stripes along the walls of the chapel. Occupying the center of the mural was an immense crucifixion scene. The face of the crucified Jesus resembled an African mask. Mary and the Apostle John flanked the cross; both were clad in African robes—Mary in orange and deep brown, John in scarlet and white. At the base of the mural was the skyline of Nairobi, including the few identifiable tall buildings in town as well as the wooden shacks of the slums. On either side of Hekima's crucifixion were two scenes from the gospel: the Multiplication of the Loaves was depicted with African women clad in green-and-blue striped dresses bearing baskets of bread, the Wedding Feast at Cana, with women carrying red clay water jugs on their heads.

A few weeks later, I mentioned this to an Ethiopian sister named Askalemariam, a member of the Little Sisters of Jesus. "I really love that chapel," I said.

"This chapel of Hekima?" said Askalemariam, screwing up her face.

"You don't like it?" I asked.

"Ah," she said with great disdain. "This chapel at Hekima is *very* ugly. What is the face of Jesus? A mask? Jesus has a mask for a face? How *foolish!*"

"But isn't it ... African?"

"Brother, it is not *my* Africa," she said. "In Ethiopia we would not paint in this way. This artist who did this is from Cameroon."

Askalemariam's pointed comment helped me to understand what some friends had been telling me all along: there was no such thing as "African" culture. Ethiopian? Sure. Kenyan? Yes. But "African?" The term is about as vague as "European."

So I decided instead to ask for stoles that might represent the styles of the refugees' home countries. I broached the subject with one of the women who ran a tailoring project.

Gaudiosa Ruzage, age thirty-five, had emigrated from Rwanda as a child along with her family in the 1960s, a victim of the Hutu-Tutsi conflicts that had long plagued her country. She was a tall, elegant woman, with delicate features, almond-shaped eyes, and a delicious sense of humor. Like many of the Rwandese in Nairobi, Gauddy, as she was known, was raised in Kenya according to the traditions of her homeland. Many Rwandese refugees lived near one another in a slum called Riruta, not too far from my Jesuit community. Laced with almost comically bumpy dirt roads that became impassable streams of mud during the rainy season, in Riruta one was just as likely to hear Kinyarwanda as Swahili or English.

Gauddy's perseverance, like that of Alice Nabwire's, was a never-ending source of amazement for me. A year earlier with one sewing machine from JRS, she had begun a small business which she called "Splendid Tailoring." Her shop was lodged on the third floor of a mud-stained concrete building in Riruta. Near the main entrance of her building was a butcher shop. Long sides of beef hung from metal ceiling hooks, and flies buzzed around the stinking carcasses.

Gauddy was an excellent seamstress and made dresses and shirts in the Central African style, with elaborately embroidered necklines, bold cotton fabrics, and flowing sleeves. In a few months Gauddy earned enough money to purchase two additional machines and organize her friends into a sort of women's cooperative. A few months later she asked the JRS scholarship program run by Sister Luise if they might consider sending her some students. Now Gauddy ran the "Splendid Tailoring Shop and School."

I broached the idea of making liturgical stoles for priests. "I have never seen these stoles, Brother," she confessed. "Perhaps you can bring one in for me to study. Then I will see if I can be making them."

The next day found Gauddy patiently studying an old stole I had borrowed from our community chapel. "Ah," she said as she fingered the green cotton fabric, "This will be very easy."

"We will start," she said confidently. "What kind of design are you wanting?

"Well, I think that the reason people will buy these stoles is that they want an African, or ... Rwandese, design," I explained tentatively.

She nodded enthusiastically. "Yes, they *will!* They *will* be buying them."

A few days later Gauddy entered my office carrying a black plastic bag. She greeted me, shook my hand, and plopped down in one of the two wooden seats in my office, wiping the sweat from her forehead. "These *matatus!*" she said, having obviously endured a crowded commute. From out of her bag she produced a number of new stoles. "I have brought you your scarves, Brother."

In a glance I could tell that the "scarves" were, unfortunately, exact replicas of the stole that I had borrowed from the Jesuit community. Plain green embroidered with white crosses. "I have made them just like the one you gave me," she said.

I labored to explain more accurately what I wanted.

"You know, Gauddy, I think that people would really be interested in something more, um, Rwandese? Am I making any sense?"

She stared at me; obviously I was making no sense. I tried again, gamely explaining what I thought I wanted. What kind of stoles did the priests wear in Rwanda? I asked. Perhaps she could use those as models.

In a few days Gauddy returned, bearing another black plastic bag. She pulled out more stoles and arranged them on the desk. "Now, I have asked some Rwandese women what I should make, Brother. And they are saying that this is the kind of scarves that the priests are wearing in Rwanda."

Not surprisingly, they were similar to the ones I had already seen. Apparently, priests in Rwanda took their fashion cues from Western missionary priests. I pulled out one from the pile. She quickly reached across the desk and pulled it back.

"Oh, Brother, that one is not completed," she said. "You see how on the back we could only find leftover material."

Gauddy turned it over to reveal a riotously colored cloth: large green and red leaves intertwined on a navy blue background. "But that's great!" I said. "What is this?"

"Oh, Brother! This?" Gauddy laughed. "This is leftover cloth for the back of the scarf! This is just *kitenge* cloth." She explained that *kitenge* was the fabric used by women for their finer dresses in Rwanda and Central Africa. "But you want scarves from this *kitenge*? Ah, these Americans will not wear this!"

Happily, Gauddy was wrong. The first *kitenge* stoles she made, in that distinctive green-and-red fabric, were sold immediately to a visiting African-American priest. He purchased ten. From the simplest design imaginable and from readily available material, Gauddy and her friends produced elegant stoles which would later turn out to be so popular that we could barely keep them in stock.

"Ah, God is good," Gauddy said quietly when I placed an order, a few days later, for another ten stoles.

Yes, God is good, I said, but why did she think so?

"Why?" Gauddy laughed and clapped her hands. "Brother!" she exclaimed. "He is helping to get rid of this leftover *kitenge*. He is giving me money for making these stoles, ones that are very easy to make. He is giving me this business for my shop and helping my ladies make money. Surely, Brother, you must be seeing that God is *very* good!"

"I Am Crying to You!"

It would be unjust to have an all-round prejudice simply because someone could deceive you. It is better to do good to several poor persons who do not deserve it than to refuse a single one who does.

—St. Claudine Thévenet

Though I soon found that I was spending all of my time working with the small business projects, I continued to work from Sister Luise's office, a few blocks from the Jesuit community. Working alongside Sister Luise and her Sudanese assistants were two highly educated, poised, and dignified Kenyan women, both named Jane. My upstairs office was an airy room with a desk, two plain wooden chairs (made by a refugee carpentry group), and a phone that worked, but only occasionally. As I began to get to know the refugees, I realized that I had little knowledge of their home countries.

"So, you've come all the way up from Sudan," I said to a Sudanese man one day.

"No, Brother Jim," he said politely, "Sudan is *up*. I have come *down*."

So I bought a huge plastic-coated map of Africa for my wall, and, for good measure, an enormous map of Nairobi. Now I could ask the refugees to point out where they had come from and where they lived in town.

BY OCTOBER THE REFUGEES in Nairobi had discovered that a new person was working with the income-generating projects. Dozens visited me at Sister Luise's office, asking for sponsorship for a business project or, more often, a little financial assistance: the man who had been locked out of his house for not paying rent; the woman who needed a few shillings to buy milk for her children. These I paid gladly, taking the money from a small petty-cash fund we kept on hand for such emergencies.

Unfortunately, it was exceedingly difficult to determine who was telling the truth and who was not, and early on I was scammed quite effectively by a number of the refugees.

One of the first refugees I helped was a young Ugandan man with a hard-luck story.

He had come to Nairobi to meet his brother, he said. They had been separated from each other in the mid-1970s during Amin's regime and hadn't seen one another since. (So far, so believable.) Unfortunately, he had no idea where his brother lived and he had come to the city with the hope of finding him. But now, he had completely failed to contact his brother. It seemed strange to me that he would travel from Uganda without knowing where his brother lived, but since neither of them had a phone, how else could he contact him but to come to Nairobi?

"And now," he said plaintively, "I am stranded." He explained he had no money to return to Kampala, no friends in Nairobi. I felt a wave of compassion for him. What an awful situation: he had not only failed to find his brother, but also was now poor and alone in Nairobi.

"And now I am *crying* to you, Brother!" He lifted his

arms heavenward. "Please, in the name of Jesus Christ, can you be giving me money to return home?"

Of course I would, I said. He smiled as he took the five hundred shilling note.

Word travels fast among the refugees. The next day another young Ugandan came to visit me.

"Brother," he said sadly, "I have just come from Uganda to visit my brother here in Nairobi. And now I have found out that he is not here. And I am stranded. You *must* be helping me Brother, I am *crying* to you!"

I mentioned this amazing coincidence to Sister Luise, who just laughed. "You are too trusting!" she said.

"The next time," Sister Luise advised, "offer to drive him to the bus station and buy a ticket for him. Then you will see how much he wants to go home."

And so, a few days later when another Ugandan man came before me and said, "Brother, I am stranded!" I questioned his story.

"But Brother," he said emphatically, "Surely, I *cannot* be making this up. I *cannot* be lying to you!"

I offered him a ride to the bus station. He regarded me for a few seconds and smiled slightly.

"Ah," he said leaning back in his chair, "You have been in Kenya for a long time, Brother?"

KAWANGWARE

The captivity of our brothers and sisters must be
reckoned as our captivity, and the grief of those
who are endangered must be esteemed as our
grief, since there is indeed one body of our
union. . . .

—St. Cyprian of Alexandria, *Letter 59*

The slums in Nairobi have names far lovelier
than they deserve: Dandora, Ngando, Mukuru,
Riruta, Ngong, Kawangware, Kibera. Some of the
names were derived from Maasai or Kikuyu words, like Mathare
or Uthiru or Kangemi. *Ngong*, for example, is the Maasai word
for "knuckles." The blue Ngong Hills themselves, visible from
many points around Nairobi, resemble the knuckles of a fist
turned toward oneself. A Maasai friend explained the story: God,
who created the great Rift Valley by scraping it out with his
hand, had left his knuckles behind after completing the task.
Nairobi itself was taken from the Maasai *Enkare Nairobi*, meaning "cold water." Many more of the neighborhoods took their

names from Swahili words: our Jesuit community was in Kili-mani, which means "in the hills."

For many months when some of the refugees spoke of their homes in "South Sea," I wondered about the exotic provenance of the neighborhood. Perhaps some retired English explorer, musing on his sojourn in the tropics, had christened this neighborhood in British East Africa. I was disappointed when, on my way to the neighborhood, I consulted my wall map of Nairobi, only to dis-cover the name was much more prosaic: South C was right next to South B, both names out of a dull city planner's imagination.

Some slum names were surprising corruptions of British colonial terms. Kariokor, a place in the northern part of Nairobi with a large open-air market, was the place where, during World War I, the British Carrier Corps was billeted. Another slum, a lit-tle farther out, was—difficult as it was to believe—the place where cars were fixed, with much banging. And so: Kariobangi.

Many of the refugees lived in clumps, near one another. The Rwandese had settled in Riruta and Dandora; Ugandans, in Ngando; Somalis, in Eastleigh; Ethiopians, in South C, Kibera, and Mathare Valley. But though the populations differed, the overall physical appearance of the various slums was remarkably similar: dirt and mud roads, choked with rotting garbage, run-ning through a warren of decrepit concrete buildings and wood-and-mud shacks with rusting, corrugated tin roofs. Everywhere there was activity: women cooking on charcoal fires in front of their homes; naked children playing beside their mothers; women with enormous pots and jerrycans balanced on their heads, strid-ing purposefully through the garbage; men passing the time talk-ing, sitting, or smoking; and a few well-dressed Kenyans on their way to their jobs downtown. Interestingly, even the residents of these neighborhoods referred to them as the "slums," a term I was initially hesitant to use for fear of giving offense.

I never felt frightened wandering through the slums, even on the numerous occasions that I found myself utterly lost amid the confusing maze of wood-and-mud shacks. Of course, my skin color marked me immediately as a "priest" or at least an aid worker. "There are only two types of white men who wander around the slums," one US Embassy worker told me at a dinner party. "Priests and CIA operatives." (Why the CIA would be exploring the slums of Nairobi I failed to ask.) Certainly the fact that I knew some Swahili helped as I *jambo*ed myself through the narrow refuse-strewn passages in search of a refugee's business or home. In any event, the predominant emotion was not fear, but pity. The sight of women standing in long snaking lines waiting for water and men wearing tattered clothes picking through garbage dumps was profoundly sorrowful. The expression *grinding* poverty never failed to come to mind when I ventured into the slums. This is what grinding poverty is, I thought; people are ground down here, like gravel underfoot.

It was well known that Nairobi in general was a violent place. During my stay, an American friend sent me an article from *The New Republic*, its title employing an expat epithet for the capital: "Nairobbery." Every day one heard tales of violence: carjackings, knifings, murders. More disturbing were tales of "mob justice," that is, Kenyans taking the law into their own hands. It was perhaps an unsurprising phenomenon, given the lack of a trustworthy legal system. The courts and judges were notoriously unreliable, the police mendacious. So for justice and the enforcement of laws, the people relied on themselves.

The results were shocking. Simply by yelling "*Mwizi!*" (Thief!) one could attract a large crowd that would chase the suspect on foot through crowded city streets, more often than not catching him, then beating him, often to death. A Jesuit priest had recently prevented someone from being killed by imploring the crowd to remember Jesus' teaching of forgiveness. The Nairobi *Daily Nation* regularly published pictures of lifeless, bruised corpses in the center of town or, similarly, from smaller outlying towns up country, thieves hanging from ropes in a dusty town square surrounded by grinning onlookers.

IN KAWANGWARE, a slum near the Jesuit community, there was a Catholic "mission parish," that is, a smaller church

connected to a larger, more established parish. Sacred Heart
Church was run by a lively Irish missionary priest named Father
Noel and a group of Franciscan Sisters. The sisters were led by
the redoubtable Sister Bernadette, who stood all of five feet tall
and had a large smile that revealed two missing front teeth.
There were many refugees living within the confines of Sacred
Heart parish, so I spoke with Sister Bernadette often. The
refugees told me she was very *mkali,* or fierce. This meant that
she expected them to be honest with her.

Sister Bernadette called me one day to inform me of a problem at Sacred Heart. A man from Kawangware had stolen some
slats of glass from the louvered windows of the small church.
"Foolishly," said Sister Bernadette, "he stole from a church."
Very foolishly, he stole in the early evening, when many people
could witness his activities in the last light of day. Members of
the neighborhood gave chase, pursuing him into the valley that
adjoins Kawangware. The mob caught the thief, killed him, cut
his arms and legs off with a machete, and left him on the ground
in a pool of blood, the broken shards of glass scattered around
his mutilated body.

News reached the pastor at Sacred Heart as he preached his
Sunday homily. From the pulpit he demanded to know the iden-
tity of the murderers. No one answered, and as Sister Bernadette
related the story, some in the congregation even spoke out to
defend their actions.

"All right," said Father Noel, "I will not continue the celebration of the Mass in this church. Instead, I will complete it in
the home of the dead man. Those who want to can follow me."
With that, he walked out of the church. Half of the parish followed, the other half did not.

After hearing stories of this nature, I was not surprised when
refugees would relate their own problems: being beaten and
jailed by police, having their wares stolen on the way to our
office, seeing their houses burnt to the ground by Kenyan neighbors. Still, I never found myself fearful. In addition to my being
recognized as a "priest" in the slums, my neighbors in Kilimani

knew me, and I imagined that I knew enough Swahili to get myself out of any difficult situation.

At night, though, I was advised to be more cautious and on the lookout for carjackers. The preferred method of night-time carjacking was as follows: A man would lie face down in the street. Naturally, you—the passing motorist—would be alarmed and stop to help. When you pulled over, two men armed with rifles would spring from the bushes and steal your car and per-haps shoot you. So what to do when someone was lying in the street? Go around him. Or, as one friend told me with a straight face, over him. I was urged *never* to pick up someone alongside the road at night. One dark night on the road to Karen I made out someone flagging me down. I drove on, passing the plaintive cries. So much for the Good Samaritan.

In time I became increasingly aware that the violence was utterly random and not confined to poor Kenyans or refugees.

AFTER JIM CORRIGAN returned from his studies in Tanzania, we both fell in with a group of young lay volunteers, with whose work and commitment I was greatly impressed.

Kevin Mestrich and Greg Darr were two Maryknoll "lay missioners" from the States who lived in a poor, rural neighbor-hood in the western part of Nairobi. Kevin worked in a sprawl-ing slum called Mukuru, near the industrial area of the city, teaching at a school run by an Irish sister. He was known as "*Mwalimu* Kevin," or Teacher Kevin, and his students and the faculty used this appellation as often as the refugees used "Brother Jim" with me. Which is to say, incessantly.

Greg worked with *Watu wa Amani*, "People for Peace," a minuscule peace-action organization. During the war in Sudan, *Watu wa Amani* brought together the warring factions at their small headquarters in Nairobi. Greg traveled throughout the country, particularly to the "land-clash" areas in western Kenya, where native Luo and Bakusu peoples had been violently forced from their land by government-backed militias. Greg helped to organize meetings with the land-clash victims and sponsored seminars on reconciliation. *Watu wa Amani,* for all of its influence, had a staff of precisely six people.

Jim Carroll, an Irish volunteer, worked in Kangemi, a Nairobi slum where the Jesuits ran a large parish. He had already worked around the world for Trócaire, an Irish volunteer agency, as a carpenter, and he now trained local Kenyans at the parish's carpentry workshop.

Mary Pat Loftus was a young American woman living with the Sisters of Notre Dame de Namur in the northern section of Nairobi, in a neighborhood populated mainly by Somali refugees. She worked in a small women's self-help group called "Maria House" in Mathare Valley.

Mathare Valley was probably the poorest section in the city, though this was the subject of long-running but somewhat facetious debate among my friends. The contest concerned which one of us worked in The Poorest Neighborhood in Nairobi. After picking my way over garbage dumps and human excrement, though, to visit Kevin at his school in Mukuru, I conceded that he had won the contest.

Along with Jim Corrigan, my fellow Jesuit, and Mark Brown, a lively Assumptionist brother who studied at Hekima, I found a reliable group of expats with whom I could laugh, share stories, and feel less lonely and less far from home.

Mary Pat had studied Swahili at the Maryknoll language school in Tanzania, and while at the school had met a gregarious Irish fellow named Niall, whom I knew slightly but admired very much. Niall worked in "the bush" at a small mission parish run by a Maasai priest. I would run into Niall at social gatherings and very occasionally in town.

One day I met him at a bank in town. I was depositing money for the JRS account; Niall was withdrawing some funds for the mission. We chatted, then he zoomed off on his motorcycle with a wave.

A few days later I learned that Niall had been killed. At a crowded memorial service in Nairobi's oldest Catholic church,

Mary Pat related the story. "There's not much to tell," she said sadly.

Niall had returned from an errand on his motorbike and pulled into the mission compound. In the far corner of the compound, he noticed some local men talking to the priest in charge. There seemed to be some sort of dispute. As Niall approached, one of the Kenyans spun around, pulled out a gun, and shot him. The bandits fled, and Niall died in a few minutes, cradled in the arms of the priest. He was twenty-five years old.

After this, I was a little more frightened, a little more careful.

"WE ARE SO GLAD YOU ARE NOT DEAD!"

Mgeni aje mwenyeji apone.
When the guest visits, the host is healed.
—Swahili proverb

Uta and I quickly realized we needed a larger place for the income-generating activities. We hoped to rent a small house in a decent neighborhood—a setting where the refugees would feel comfortable visiting us and where we could also attract customers for the refugees' products. After contacting a number of real estate agents in town, we found what we thought would be a perfect place in a tony neighborhood called Lavington: a sprawling mansion with parquet wood floors, a red-tiled roof, and a broad, sunny porch. The main rooms were large enough to accommodate display cases and tables for a showroom. We could easily imagine refugees congregating on the porch and visitors wandering around the grounds.

But between all of the searching for a new place, driving

back and forth between the slums, and meeting with dozens of refugees, I found myself worn out. The refugees started to tell me I was looking "poorly." "*Umechoka sana*, Brother?" Are you very tired?

One morning I woke with a sore throat. A Jesuit physician with whom I lived suggested that it was probably just a virus, a reasonable diagnosis since the refugees themselves were invariably sick. Doubtless I had picked something up at work.

The conditions in which the refugees lived conspired to keep them continually unwell. First of all, many of the refugees had either contracted HIV, were living with full-blown AIDS, or were married to someone with the virus. Every day in the *Daily Nation* there appeared dozens of mournful obituaries, accompanied by pictures of young men and women, having died "after a long illness bravely borne." The disease that has touched the lives of almost every Kenyan is known there as *ukimwi*, an abbreviation for *ukosefu kinga mwili*, that is, a body without protection. (Kevin Mestrich told me his young students asserted that "AIDS" itself stood for *[H]atari Imeingia Duniani Sasa*: danger that has now entered the world.)

Despite its prevalence, however, *ukimwi* was not discussed as openly in Kenya as in neighboring Uganda. There were a number of reasons for this reluctance. First, illness in general is rarely discussed as freely as it is in the States; Kenyans consider such information to be highly personal. Another major reason was fear. It was estimated at the time that in certain areas of the country upwards of 30 percent of the population carried the HIV virus—though this figure was notoriously difficult to verify. (The Kenyan government refrains from publicly mentioning the disease for fear of harming the tourist industry.) One way of dealing with the illness, then, was a sort of denial; the less Kenyans are reminded about it, the less they worry. Finally, AIDS was often considered a "dirty" disease akin to gonorrhea or syphilis, or worse—in rural areas and urban slums *ukimwi* was sometimes seen as a curse from the spiritual world. This was true for Christians, Muslims, and those practicing traditional religions.

In addition to the debilitating HIV virus, the sanitary conditions in the slums—no running water, often no clean water at all, foul stagnant pools of garbage and human excrement—were effective breeding grounds for all sorts of germs. The lack of clean water, for example, meant that diarrhea was a great danger in Nairobi, particularly for children. Dysentery, tuberculosis, influenza, malaria, mumps, and hepatitis were all common among those who lived in the slums. Soon after my arrival two hundred people in eastern Kenya died from meningitis, something that a simple vaccination could have prevented. When I read about the epidemic I remembered my own vaccination against meningitis: a simple pinprick, costing only a few dollars. In point of fact, it was free for me—covered by my generous insurance provider. It seemed profoundly unjust that something so readily available in the States was unavailable here—where it was most desperately needed and where it could easily have saved hundreds of lives.

There were rarely toilets in any of the refugees' shacks. Houses in the slums had no heating, and during the rainy season, when the temperature could dip into the forties and fifties, warm clothes were difficult to come by. Poverty made it difficult for the refugees to buy healthy food for themselves and their children. Their lives were also replete with stress—worrying about the future, remembering the past—and full of hard work—walking many miles with children on their backs to the water pump, to market, to aid agencies looking for some help. The refugees were often beaten by the Kenyan police, locked out of their homes by capricious landlords, thrown off of city buses, and sometimes harassed by their neighbors. It was heartbreaking to know people who were *always* suffering and ill. "Somehow I am a little sick today, Brother," was a constant refrain, so I tried as far as possible to put my own very minor physical concerns in perspective.

But after a few days of ignoring my own condition, my throat grew worse, and I found it difficult to do any work. Jim Corrigan drove me to Nairobi Hospital. It was reputed to be one of the best hospitals in the region, but among picky expats it had something less than a stellar reputation. (One local joke ran as follows: What's the best hospital in East Africa? British Airways.)

Jim and I waited an hour in a small reception room marked with a chipped wooden sign reading "Casualty Dept." This room, I would later discover in Richard Preston's medical thriller *The Hot Zone*, was where one of the first Ebola patients was brought in 1980, only to die (precisely where we were now sitting) a horrifying death. The author describes the setting:

> *It is a small room lined with padded benches. The clear, strong ancient light of East Africa pours through a row of windows and falls across a table heaped with soiled magazines, and makes rectangles on a pebbled grey floor that has a drain in its center. The room smells vaguely of wood smoke and sweat and it is jammed with bleary-eyed people, Africans and Europeans sitting shoulder to shoulder.*

We shared our bench with a few Kenyans coughing and wiping their running noses, and a man who described for us how his plane had crashed in the Maasai Mara Game Reserve. He was bleeding profusely from a gash on his forehead and tried gamely to staunch the bleeding with his wife's handkerchief. "Bad luck!" he kept saying over and over, like a mantra.

After a few minutes a Kenyan doctor led me to a small compartment in the busy emergency room. I climbed onto a rickety wooden table and waited a bit longer. He returned with another nurse, whom he referred to as "sister" in British fashion. (For a brief moment I thought she was a nun.) The doctor drew the stained cotton curtains as I explained my situation.

"Say ah," he said. He looked.

"I am going to give you a shot," he decided. "If you get any sicker, come back and see me."

I grimaced. Getting any sort of shot in East Africa was, according to even the most optimistic sources, ill advised, given the perfectly reasonable fear of AIDS. But I had little choice. In any event, the shot did no good; my throat grew worse, and my fever climbed. I returned the next day to find an Indian doctor. "Hmm ... say ah." He considered my throat.

"Here are some pills," he said, reaching into a cabinet mounted on the wall. I looked at the bottle of erythromycin. "Take these and see what happens," he said. "If you get any sicker, come back and see me." (I wondered if that last sentence was part of some sort of script given out to Nairobi doctors.)

Falling ill in Africa was my biggest fear. The cultural aspects of working in Kenya—language, food, new customs, and so on—did not worry me. Nor did the simplicity of lifestyle. Nor did the distance from home. Nor did the lack of communication. But sickness was definitely worrisome. I spoke to a Jesuit friend about this a few months before leaving. "Remember that getting sick is part of the experience of working overseas, too," he said. It was also considered something of a value among the missionaries to stick with local doctors, as another way of more fully sharing in the life of those with whom you worked. On the other hand, the Americans I knew at the US Embassy avoided them like the plague. Instead, they simply waited until they returned home or saw an American doctor at the embassy. But I agreed with my missionary friends. It hardly seemed right on the one hand to profess a simple lifestyle and on the other to run off to expensive Western doctors at the first sign of illness.

Still and all, it was hard not to be a little worried.

The next morning I found it difficult to breathe. I returned to another doctor. "Erythromycin?" he said contemptuously. "This will not work. Take these pills." Ampicillin. That night I woke with severe pains in my stomach and chest, and I vomited. Jim looked on in horror. "I thought you were having a heart attack," he said the next morning as we drove to the hospital.

The fourth doctor asked me to hop up onto an examining table.

"Well!" he exclaimed. "This throat is *very* red. If it gets any more swollen, I will have to cut it."

"*Cut it?*" I asked.

"Yes, or you will not be able to breathe," he said evenly.

Though I was still baffled by the prognosis, I was confident that I did not want my throat cut. So, inculturation or no, I asked my Jesuit superior if he knew any American doctors. He put me in touch with the chief doctor of the Peace Corps in Nairobi. The Peace Corps office in town faced Jevanjee Gardens, near the nicer youth hostels. Apple-cheeked young Americans sat in his waiting room—Peace Corps volunteers, I assumed. On the secretary's desk sat an enormous glass bowl filled with condoms.

The doctor was a young man I had met sometime earlier in the year.

"Say ah," he said.

"You have strep throat," he said, tossing away the tongue depressor. "And you probably have mono, too. You'll need to get a test. Here's the place I send everyone." He gave me a prescription for penicillin.

My second needle in a week, I thought, as I drove to the address he had given me. I wondered if the needle would be sterile. The Kenyan nurse sensed my unease. "I know you Americans are very concerned with your needles," she said. "So I will open it in front of you. See . . . " She noisily peeled away plastic from a new needle. Rather than consoling me, it terrified me. Had I seen them unwrap a clean needle at the hospital? I couldn't remember.

In a few days my sore throat subsided, but on March 15 I received the results of the tests: mononucleosis, or "glandular fever" as they say in East Africa. Nothing to do but bed rest, said Dr. Peace Corps.

I remained in bed for two months. At this point there was no television in our little community, so I made do with old books, reading everything I could get my hands on. There were, I knew, refugees and Kenyans who were much sicker than I was, and I knew that eventually I would recover. But I was miserable nonetheless.

St. Thérèse of Lisieux, the French Carmelite, made some pointed observations about the value of hardship in her autobiography, *The Story of a Soul*, which I read during my recovery.

She believed that in suffering, by placing our trust in God, we may come to be stronger and wiser:

> *A child whom a doctor wants to perform a painful operation on, will not fail to utter loud cries and say that the remedy was worse than the sickness; however, when he is cured a few days later he is happy at being able to play and run. It is the same for souls; soon they recognize that a little bitterness is at times preferable to sugar.*

A good insight, but one that was almost impossible, I found at the time, to internalize.

It was without a doubt the low point of my time in Nairobi. Though I enjoyed my work, I wasn't sure if I had been able to contribute all that much. I also had to admit that even after six months, I missed my friends and family back home as much as ever, and I knew that my being away was especially difficult for my parents. Two years apart was a big thing to ask, they had said sadly. Before I had left for Nairobi I expressed my concern to a Jesuit priest, who had spent many years working overseas, that my parents might miss me overly. "Don't worry," he said brightly, "God takes special care of the parents of missionaries!" That sounded reasonable. After all, I figured it was the *least* God could do, as I was attempting to follow "God's will" and all that, and making what I considered to be a not-insignificant sacrifice.

That same week, I received news that my father had suffered what his doctors called a transient ischemic attack, a sort of "mini-stroke," which had left him temporarily paralyzed. I felt utterly helpless. Telephone calls home were painful for both of us, and I wept when I hung up the phone. Through the crackling transatlantic line I could hear my father's somewhat slurred speech and my mother's brave attempts to lessen my worries. I grew angry with God and said as much in prayer. How could God not take care of my family, as I expected and had asked him to?

At the time, the image that came most frequently in prayer was that of Joseph in the well, from the book of Genesis. That was how I felt: stuck at the absolute bottom of a deep, dry well, uncertain and doubtful of what lay ahead in the future.

Perhaps, I thought, returning home would be the best thing to do. I wondered, for example, how I would be able to recover fully if I were to be working around people who were sick themselves. Maybe my parents needed me more than the refugees. Maybe my first responsibility was to them.

My Jesuit superiors offered me the option of returning to the States. I even thought of going home for a short stay, perhaps a few months, but I was sure that if I left Kenya at that point, I would not come back—such was my state of mind. In the end, tempting as it was to leave I decided that I owed it to the refugees to stay. Though I didn't feel that I had yet been able to help them very much, they seemed to rely on me and trust me anyway. And I was, I discovered during my convalescence, growing fond of the refugees. I missed seeing them every day.

It was also rather clear to me, even at the time, that these types of experiences helped me, even if in a small way, better to appreciate the experiences of the refugees. It would be ridiculous, of course, to equate my admittedly minor illness with the serious diseases they suffered. What was mono next to AIDS or cholera or typhoid? Or to say that missing my parents who were, after all, safe at home was equivalent to missing a child who had died in a refugee camp or mourning a relative one would never see again. Or that my being away from home for two years was the same as leaving one's homeland forever. Still, I found that my own small struggles made me want to help the refugees even more. Strangely—or maybe not so strangely— I felt my compassion for them increase dramatically. I *couldn't* leave. So I stayed.

FORTUNATELY FOR BOTH my spiritual and physical health, two sweet, elderly Maryknoll sisters lived across the street. The Maryknoll Sisters, a congregation of adventurous women, was founded by the effervescent Mary Rogers, a graduate of Smith College who had worked in China during the early part of the century. In Penny Lernoux's story of the Maryknoll Sisters, *Hearts on Fire*, there is a captivating photograph of Mother Mary Rogers facing the title page. The photograph frames an enormous woman, in a billowing black habit and long veil. Her mouth is open; the camera clearly catches Mary Rogers in the middle of a booming laugh. One hand, slightly blurred, is making a sweeping gesture, perhaps toward an unseen friend; in the other hand she holds a Bible. It is a delightful picture, and one that neatly captures the generous spirituality of her order.

Claire Murphy and Eileen Kelly ran a guest house called Villa Rogers for the Maryknoll sisters who worked in Kenya, southern Sudan, and northern Tanzania. (There were numerous Maryknoll fathers in East Africa as well.) The two had worked in Tanzania for decades, and they took it upon themselves to look after Jim Corrigan and me. We were often invited to their home for Mass, a home-cooked meal, and some motherly advice. While I was cooped up with mono, Eileen, an experienced nurse who had seen far worse in her time in Africa, would drop by and offer encouragement. "Oh, you'll be *fine.*"

My other frequent visitors were from a delightful community who lived a hundred meters away, the Little Sisters of Jesus. Their order was founded by Charles de Foucauld, a Frenchman who, early in the twentieth century, took up the life of a hermit in the North African desert. The spirituality of the Little Sisters (there were Little Brothers, too) centered on the Catholic tradition of the "hidden life" of Jesus, that is, the period of Jesus' life that goes unrecorded in the gospels, from his discovery in the Temple—around age twelve—to the beginning of his public ministry at age thirty. In essence, during those years Jesus lived like anyone else in first-century Palestine, with his small family, learning and perfecting the trade of carpentry with his father. The hidden life of Jesus, then, is nothing more than the common life. So the Little Brothers and Sisters live the hidden life, working among regular people in regular jobs—as maids, factory workers, seamstresses, janitors.

I first had occasion to meet the Little Sisters when an

Ethiopian Jesuit visiting Loyola House asked me to carry an Amharic Bible to two of their Ethiopian sisters.

An African sister swung open the high iron gate after I rang the bell. Like the rest of her sisters, she wore a royal blue wraparound skirt, a powder blue blouse and a simple kerchief tied around her head. She greeted me—a total stranger—effusively.

"Oh, we are so glad you have come!"

As I followed her up the path I saw that their tiny green-and-white bungalow was surrounded by a flourishing garden. Pale blue irises, clumps of magenta and white bougainvillea bushes, emerald-green hibiscus bushes with lipstick-red flowers, wild sisal plants, tall Norfolk pines, sweet-smelling frangipani and gardenia bushes, and orange day lilies that nodded in the hot sun, all were well cared for by the Little Sisters.

Inside the house that day was the entire community of nine. Their superior—a French sister named Monique who smiled constantly—a Maltese sister, a Nigerian sister, two Tanzanian sister, two Kenyan sisters, and two Ethiopian sisters. The nine rushed to greet me at the door. When I presented the Bible to the two Ethiopian sisters, they lavished praise on me for my great act of charity (which consisted of walking all of two blocks with a book).

Sister Askalemariam, one of the Ethiopian sisters (whose name, she said, meant "Gift of Mary") gave me a tour of their house, which began at their chapel—a small shack with a tin roof—which lay behind their living quarters. Arching over the chapel was a tall tree whose berries, falling from a considerable height, dropped on the tin roof with a sound not unlike gunshots. Inside were low pine benches surrounding a simple altar covered with an embroidered cloth. Placed in front of the altar was a small unpainted ceramic statue of the Child Jesus. Askalemariam bowed to the altar.

They begged me to stay and cheerfully fixed me tea and biscuits. The entire community, setting their tasks aside, sat down and chatted. I was reminded of a passage in the Gospel of Luke, when Jesus visits the home of his friends Martha and Mary.

Martha was working diligently preparing a meal, while her sister Mary spent her time simply relaxing and chatting with Jesus. Not surprisingly, Martha complains to Jesus about her sister. "Martha, Martha," he says in reply, "you worry about so much. But only one thing is necessary. Mary has chosen the better part." The Little Sisters knew how to work hard like Martha, but also how to relax like Mary.

Their joy was infectious. The Little Sisters laughed *constantly*—about anything, or so it seemed. Making silly jokes about one another, about their community, their studies, their superior. Sister Monique laughed loudest of all when they teased her about her French cooking (which, I gathered, the East African sisters found mystifying). They listened intently as I described the kind of work I was doing with the refugees. Then Sister Monique announced, "Brother, you will be coming to visit us *often.*"

I did, frequently. The home-cooked food, I have to admit, was a decided attraction. But far more important was the deep joy I experienced in their community. Living simply, with no phone, no electricity (all cooking was done over charcoal or on a kerosene stove) and, like the rest of Nairobi, very little water, they seemed not to mind. They seemed in fact to like it.

A few months later, two friends from the States arrived for a visit, and we drove past by the Little Sisters' house in my jeep. Having just returned from Sunday Mass, the sisters were gathered outside of the gate of their house. They flagged me down. When I stopped they surrounded the car like bees around a flower.

"Brother, Brother! *Jambo sana!*" they shouted. "Who are your friends?"

Since in East Africa one always shook hands when meeting someone, dozens of small hands were thrust through the open windows of the little jeep, waiting to be shaken.

"Hello! Hello! *Jambo sana!*" they said between peals of laughter. "We are the Little Sisters of Jesus!"

My astonished friends were confronted with nine giggling women in blue habits and a flurry of hands. "What the hell was *that?*" one of them asked as we drove away.

The Little Sisters and I became great friends, so I was not surprised when Sister Askalemariam and Sister Mariam dropped by to visit me. Visiting the sick—one of the "corporal works of mercy" in the Christian tradition—was taken very seriously in East Africa. While in the States one might leave a sick friend alone (to recover) or perhaps phone him, here it was considered rude *not* to visit and, not incidentally, help out around the house. Besides, how could you call if you had no telephone?

Sisters Mariam and Askalemariam spent time with me, sipping orange Fantas, telling me what was going on with Sister Monique and the Little Sisters. "When will you be coming to dinner again?"

Refugees, too, visited constantly. At times I was overwhelmed by fatigue and would have preferred simply to rest. Nevertheless, I was grateful for their visits, and I found it nothing short of astonishing that the refugees had discovered where I lived. I knew they would never have given out my address at the JRS office. (In the past, some refugees, having discovered where one of the JRS workers lived, visited his house days, nights, and weekends.) But somehow my refugee friends knew, and they came. To visit, to chat, and, in the custom of East Africa, to clean the house. Two Ugandan refugees dropped by the house late one afternoon while I took my *pumzika*, my nap.

"Brother Jim! Brother Jim!" they tapped on my bedroom window, and I leaped out of bed, dazed and confused.

"Get up! We are here!"

For the next hour I sat on a stool in the kitchen, trying not to doze off, while they chatted about other refugees, swept the kitchen floor, and washed my breakfast dishes.

Otherwise I stayed in bed and read. Gradually I felt well enough to wander around the house, walk a block down to the main Jesuit community, and occasionally drive into town for medicine.

My first day back in the jeep, I drove to the local pharmacy for a refill of vitamins. Two women by the side of the road flagged me down. "Brother! Brother!"

I had absolutely no idea who they were, but by this point I was accustomed to being recognized by refugees throughout the city. "There are one hundred thousand refugees in Nairobi," said Sister Luise when I arrived, "and soon they will all know you."

I pulled the car over, stretched over and rolled down the window on the passenger side. The two women, Rwandese, stuck their heads in the car and laughed.

"Oh Brother!" one exclaimed. "You are recovered! We are so glad you are not dead!"

MIKONO

The wilderness and the dry land shall be glad,
the desert shall rejoice and blossom.
Like the crocus it shall blossom abundantly,
and rejoice with joy and singing.

—Isaiah 35:1-2

After I got back on my feet, Uta and I began again to look in earnest for a suitable house. This proved more difficult than either of us had anticipated. If we located a house in a reasonably safe neighborhood, we would discover that we weren't permitted to use it as a "shop." (This was the fate of the house in Lavington that we had admired a few months earlier.) If we heard of a house that could be used as a shop, we would discover that it was situated on an inaccessible road, making visits from tourists unlikely. The search continued for some months, with an energetic Uta driving a listless me around the city in her Range Rover. It seemed that every time we drew close to signing a lease, a complication would arise.

But in the meantime we hit upon a fortunate place to sell our goods: the United States Embassy in Nairobi. A woman I had met at a dinner party suggested that I contact the "Community Liaison Officer," whose job it was to connect the embassy staff with the city in which they lived. Lynn, the CLO, told me that every few weeks she ran a small bazaar inside the embassy to showcase local handicrafts. Would I be interested in running one? Of course I would.

Uta and I contacted the refugees to let them know what kinds of goods we would like to collect. We focused on items that visitors to our offices seemed to like best: Rwandese sisal baskets with bold geometric patterns, stuffed animals, animals carved from ebony, Ethiopian paintings, embroidered T-shirts, Rwandese grass lampshades, wooden jewelry boxes, and note cards with dried banana-leaf designs. Césaire Mukamwiza Kanjoui, a highly educated Rwandese woman who had earned a master's degree in nursing in Belgium, now made her living stringing beaded necklaces. We purchased fifty in preparation for our visit to the embassy. Jane Tusiime, a young Ugandan woman, stitched pillow cases and purses made from barkcloth, a product gained by stripping bark from fig trees and pounding it until it takes on the consistency of a rough, mahogany-colored cloth. Mary Kabiito, another Ugandan, bought inexpensive leather bags in the markets of Nairobi and painted them with fantastic designs in pastel colors: swirling paisley shapes, animals, flowers, and human faces. The week before the bazaar our office resembled a small warehouse, with T-shirts and dresses piled high on the bookcases, a line of carved animals marching resolutely across the floor behind my desk, and towers of baskets piled precariously on the rusty filing cabinets.

On the morning of the bazaar Uta and I stuffed everything into her Range Rover and headed downtown. Gauddy accompanied us; Uta and I thought that the experience of selling to Americans would be valuable if she ever decided to expand her own business. After we passed through the high iron gates surrounding the embassy, two tall Marines searched our car, first peering under the hood of the Range Rover, and then sticking a long mirror under the car.

"They're checking to see if we have bombs," Uta whispered. With US troops stationed in Somalia, there had been numerous threats on the Americans in Nairobi. The embassy's security concerns also extended to our products; they inspected each doll, each carved animal, each necklace, and each lampshade with a small metal detector that hummed and clicked ominously.

Upstairs, Lynn had procured two long tables in a large meeting room. After an hour of work the conference room looked almost like a shop. At noon dozens of Americans came in. It had been a while since I had seen so many white faces. My first thought was, Am I really that pale?

Uta and I hoped the Americans might buy at least a few of our things; it was a few weeks before Easter—a good time to sell things, according to Lynn.

Items flew from the table. We had, for example, brought patchwork quilts made by a trio of Ugandan women who called themselves the *Agali Awamu* group. Led by a cheerful and hardworking woman named Halima Mutebe, the three visited fabric shops in Nairobi and requested leftover scraps of *kitenge*. Using these cheap scraps they stitched together magnificent patchwork quilts that would have sold for hundreds of dollars in the States.

The first American woman to enter the room strode directly to the patchwork quilts and asked me the price. Uta glanced at me. We had disagreed on prices for the refugees' handicrafts. I wanted to keep them very low. Uta, based on her experience in India, argued for a higher price. If prices were too low, she explained, people will think that your handicrafts are cheaply made. I took a breath and took Uta's advice: "Fifty dollars for the twin size, and one hundred for the double."

"I'll take them all," she said, scooping up a mountain of fabric. Uta smiled beatifically. Gauddy stared at me with wide eyes.

We sold all of the baskets, all of the carved animals. The Americans took every embroidered T-shirt, every jewelry box, every carved lampstand, and every straw lampshade. Sarah Nakate, a Ugandan refugee, had made six dozen white cotton napkins embroidered with green elephants, red lions, violet sunbirds, and black-and-white zebras. They disappeared in the first fifteen minutes, and we found ourselves with orders for six more sets. Jane Tusiime's barkcloth designs and Mary Kabiito's leather bags were similarly snapped up. The only leftovers were a few note cards and the odd necklace.

Since we had no need to charge overhead, our prices were unbeatable, and the cagey American embassy types knew it. Our goods were also more eclectic than the standard fare found in the markets of Nairobi, which featured only Kenyan-made items. Unlike those stores, our goods came from all over East Africa— Ethiopia, Rwanda, Mozambique, Uganda, Sudan, and Somalia. Our new American customers were very excited, as were we. Needless to say, the refugees were overjoyed. "We should visit the American embassy every day!" one of them said hopefully. All of this convinced us that a shop would be a success.

JOHN GUINEY, a Jesuit who ran a parish in Kangemi, a near-by slum, mentioned in passing one day that the parish owned a vacant house a few meters away from the church. I remembered seeing the place, a decent enough house, but I wondered about the location. Kangemi was a violent neighborhood, notorious even in Nairobi for its burglaries and murders. Despite this, Uta and I agreed to take a look at the house.

Kangemi lies on the western edge of Nairobi, along the road to Nakuru. It is a strange amalgam of urban and rural poverty: wooden shacks with tin roofs; decrepit, mud-stained concrete buildings; and a patchwork of *shambas*, or small farms, of corn and long green cowgrass. Ten years earlier, the Jesuits had taken over a "mission" parish there, that is, a parish for a small village associated with a larger, neighboring church. Bit by bit, the small parish had grown.

The Jesuits in Kangemi viewed the growth of the parish according to one of the tenets of liberation theology, which recognizes that God works in the church not only through the clergy but through the laity as well. They arranged the parish into "small Christian communities," groups of families organized by neighborhood. Whereas in the past a missionary pastor might have managed the parish autocratically, the Catholic parishioners in Kangemi were involved in nearly every aspect of parish planning.

In just three years the parishioners had erected an immense, red brick, A-frame church on a plot overlooking the wide Kangemi valley. It took for its name one of the traditional ones for Jesus' foster father: St. Joseph the Worker, or *Mtakatifu Yosefu Mfanyakazi*. The name also honored all who labor.

The church's vast concrete floor, with its dull, red, iron-oxide paint, echoed many public buildings in the country. Its grey granite stones were cut from a local quarry. A huge crucifix with a jet-black Jesus presided at the end of the nave. Flanking the cross were icons of Mary and Joseph, both depicted as Africans. On the walls, encircling rows of simple wooden slat benches, ran the fifteen "Stations of the Cross," which also depicted Jesus as an African. The structure itself had been designed by a Belgian Jesuit, but when John Guiney gave tours of the church, he never failed to note that each brick, each tile, and each beam had been made by people in the parish.

The parishioners in Kangemi took a tremendous amount of pride in their church. Sunday Masses were an all-morning affair; the back doors of the church were flung open to provide viewing for hundreds seated in an outdoor amphitheater behind the church. St. Joseph the Worker was itself a small village within Kangemi. From its modest beginnings the church's works expanded to include a carpentry shop, a computer learning center, a tile-making shop, a printing press, and, of course, a school. All were run by local Kenyans. A Catholic women's religious order, the Missionary Sisters of Our Lady of Africa, ran a medical clinic, or "dispensary," in the parish. The sisters had also founded a small income-generating shop—now managed by neighborhood women—that produced cunningly designed cloth figures dressed in traditional Kenyan styles: Kikuyu dolls, Maasai dolls, Kamba dolls. Their shop was called Dollicraft.

Despite the Jesuit presence in Kangemi, Uta knew the area

far better than I did, the result of her many visits to refugees who lived there. So one day we climbed into Uta's Range Rover and took off to Kangemi for a look at the house. John suggested that we talk to the superior of the sisters, since the house had previously been used by a lay nurse who worked at their dispensary.

On an earlier visit to Kangemi, months before, I met one of the sisters. Walking along a dirt path with John, we bumped into a smiling young woman, quite obviously European or American, with short brown hair and glasses. "Hi! I'm Sister Bernice!" she said brightly. "And I'm a White Sister!"

Words failed me. I thought she had said she was a "white sister," rather than a "White Sister." My embarrassed expression told her of my confusion, and Sister Bernice laughed.

Sister Bernice's order had been known, until quite very recently, as the "White Sisters," a nickname that referred to their sisters' habits, not their skin color. But as more African vocations joined their congregation, the sisters had deemed it prudent to gently remind people of their original name: The Missionary Sisters of Our Lady of Africa, a real mouthful that was usually reduced to the MSOLA Sisters. The White Fathers faced a similar problem. But their situation had proven even more complicated, because their order included not only Africans, but also many men who were not ordained. As one of the White Fathers explained to me, "You can be a black Brother and still be a White Father!" They stopped using their common name in 1984, returning their congregation to its original name: The Missionaries of Africa. Still, any mention of, say, the new MSOLA nomenclature was invariably followed by a helpful "you know—the White Sisters."

The sisters' building turned out to be perfect for our needs: a one-story bungalow with a tiled roof, a broad porch, large airy rooms, and a big back yard. The reasonable rent, Uta and I discovered, would be used by the parish for a fund for unwed mothers. So the money given to JRS by the donor agencies would be doubly blessed: used first for the refugees and then for single mothers.

After signing the papers we set to work immediately—and discovered, happily, that much of the work could be done by the refugee enterprises. Uta and I, for example, wanted the front porch to be a waiting area and gathering space for the refugees, so we asked Joseph Semakula, a Ugandan refugee with a furniture shop in Kangemi, to make sturdy wooden benches. He also constructed an immense display table and four tall bookshelves from sweet-smelling pine for the living room, which would serve as the shop itself. For a back bedroom, which would become an office for Uta and me, he built two small pine desks.

One concern about our move stood out: how would the refugees find us? They had no phones or post office boxes and moved (or "shifted," as they would say) frequently. Perhaps we should send out some sort of notice, but how? Or maybe Sister Luise should tell them.

We had, of course, forgotten about the exceedingly efficient refugee grapevine. Within three days of our move, twenty refugees appeared, having already heard that we needed handicrafts to fill our store. Dozens showed up over the next few weeks, lugging sisal baskets, beaded jewelry, straw mats, patchwork quilts, embroidered T-shirts, carved wooden lampstands, paintings, stuffed animals, batik-print fabrics and woven sisal purses called *kiondos*. In two weeks we were fully stocked and ready for business. Thereafter, visits from twenty or thirty refugees a day was the norm.

WHAT COULD WE CALL IT? I was already thinking about marketing; we needed a name that was catchy and easy to remember. And it was important to use a name that the refugees would like. Initially I wanted to name the place in honor of a famous Jesuit. Pedro Arrupe, the charismatic superior general of the Society of Jesus from 1965 to 1983 and founder of the Jesuit Refugee Service, immediately came to mind.

"What about the Arrupe Center?" I suggested to Mike Evans, JRS director for East Africa.

Mike groaned and told me a story. His predecessor, not too

many years ago, had also named a refugee center in Nairobi after Father Arrupe. This Arrupe Center offered handouts of a few hundred shillings a person for indigent refugees. In time the place was overwhelmed with hundreds of people and was forced to close down. My boss thought that refugees might assume that our new office and shop was also a place for handouts. So, no second Arrupe Center.

What about naming it after a Jesuit saint? I liked that idea (though I wasn't sure how Uta, a Lutheran, would feel about it). St. Ignatius of Loyola was the founder of the Society of Jesus. The main Jesuit community, however, was already called Loyola House, and tradition mitigated against two identically named houses, for fear of sowing confusion among Jesuits. There was also a Xavier House in Kampala, after the great Jesuit missionary, St. Francis Xavier, and a Campion House in Nairobi, after the English martyr St. Edmund Campion. I was running out of Jesuit saints.

With Joseph's pine benches in place, the refugees began congregating on the porch every morning at nine o'clock, waiting for Uta and me to arrive. One morning I asked them for some advice. What about naming this place for an African saint?

That was a good idea, they said.

The most famous of the East African saints were the Ugandan Martyrs, a group of twelve or so young boys who were killed by the *kabaka,* the king of the Baganda people, in the late nineteenth century. The young boys, pages to the king, had been baptized as Christians only a few months before their deaths. A number of parish communities were named after one or another of the martyrs.

"What about Kizito?" I asked, naming the youngest boy. I liked the name, it was easy to remember.

Three Ugandan women who ran the quilt-making project nodded vigorously. "That is wonderful, Brother!"

At the same time I noticed a Sudanese woman seated on another bench, scowling. "Brother, what about Bakhita?" she asked. Bakhita was a recently canonized Sudanese woman, a member of the Canossian Sisters.

Now the Ugandans scowled. Any "African" saint would mean, at least in the eyes of the refugees, honoring only one country. So, no African saints, for fear of divisiveness.

Maybe a simple Swahili word would be better, I thought. In that case, perhaps the word for something like "hope" or "faith." I located a Swahili dictionary.

"How about *Mwangaza?*" for light. "That's the name of the Jesuit retreat house in Nairobi," one of my community members reminded me.

"*Tumaini?*" for hope? Nope, already taken by a women's religious order that ran a small community nearby.

"*Hekima?*" for wisdom? The Jesuit theology school in Nairobi.

"*Imani?*" for faith? Now it was Uta's turn to groan. She explained that the Kenyan president's political party, the Kenyan African National Unity party, used the word regularly for naming public buildings and the like. So much for Swahili. We were getting desperate, and a refugee suggested something even simpler. "What about something like *mikono?*" for hands. That sounded good: short and easy to remember, especially for American and European ears. I suggested it to the refugees the next day.

"*Mikono?*" Why are you calling it "hands?" I explained the shop would showcase the work of their hands and that everyone would be working hand in hand. "Ahhh!" Gauddy Ruzage said. "That is *very* good!"

But not everyone was pleased. "The Ugandan Martyrs," said one of the Ugandans, "would have been better."

We hired three people to work alongside us: Virginia Gatonye, a young Kenyan woman, would be our cleaning woman; Marie Bugwiza, a Rwandese refugee, our saleswoman; and Berehe, an elderly Ethiopian man, our groundskeeper.

Slowly we began attracting customers. Priests and religious began dropping by, as well as friends from the American Embassy. In a few weeks, we were up to at least three or four customers a day. In time, the Mikono Centre's customers expanded to include expatriates, diplomats, long-time British "settlers," wealthy Kenyans, missionary clergy, Peace Corps workers, and American and European tourists hunting for bargains.

We opened the shop, officially that is, on August 28 with an outdoor Mass celebrated by the Catholic archbishop of Nairobi, His Eminence Maurice Cardinal Otunga, a tall, stately Kenyan prelate. In the course of the preparations I discovered in the Sacramentary (the Catholic church's compendium of liturgical prayers) a "Mass for Refugees and Exiles," which the cardinal agreed would be a fine choice for the occasion.

Gauddy and the rest of the Splendid Tailoring group, who were by now quite adept at making religious vestments, fashioned a special emerald-green stole for the cardinal. The altar linens were refugee-made batiks in greens and blacks; the chalice, a carved wooden cup made by Mozambiquan refugees; the paten, a sisal basket woven by Rwandese women. As I sat in the back yard during the Mass, in the cool shade of an avocado tree, surrounded by dozens of refugees singing songs in Swahili, Kinyarwanda, French, and English, I realized how happy I was that I had stayed in Nairobi.

Cardinal Otunga's homily commented on the readings from Exodus and from the Gospel of Matthew, using a passage known as the Flight to Egypt. He reminded us that Mary, Joseph, and Jesus, fleeing the murderous King Herod, were themselves refugees. After the cardinal completed his thirty-five-minute homily, one refugee leaned over to me and said, "Brother, this bishop must like us *very* much if he is speaking to us for so long." Afterwards the cardinal sprinkled the front porch with holy water and prayed a blessing for the Mikono Centre.

ALL IN ALL, THE HOUSE in Kangemi proved to be a perfect setup: The refugees had a place to congregate and market their goods. Though it was located in one of the poorest slums of Nairobi, it was easily accessible by car (for customers) and by *matatu* (for the refugees). And given the arrangement of the house, customers could meet and talk with the refugees sitting on the porch outside. Uta and I had found an office for ourselves, and could now spend much more time helping the refugees with their problems, and, more importantly, listening to their stories.

STORIES FROM THE GRASS

Wapiganapo tembo nyasi huumia.
When the elephants fight, it is the grass that suffers.
—Swahili proverb

Kiiza John Francis, a Ugandan refugee, appeared at the Mikono Centre one morning in a filthy T-shirt and a robin's-egg-blue sweater with a long tear in one sleeve. He had a placid face and a soft voice. He was very thin. Kiiza's story, though difficult to believe at first, was subsequently corroborated by other Ugandans. "Kiiza has had a hard life," one of them whispered to me. Kiiza related his story deliberately, with a glassy-eyed stare.

He was a young man living in a small village in eastern Uganda during the dictatorship of Idi Amin Dada. In 1979, during Amin's war against the Tanzanian-backed Ugandan National Liberation Front (UNLF), Kiiza was drafted into the Ugandan army. Kiiza's unit was sent to fight against the UNLF rebels in Tanzania. TZ, the East Africans call Tanzania, pronouncing it as the English do: "T-Zed." Kiiza was seventeen at the time and left behind a young wife.

He fought bravely in TZ, he said, but was captured by the UNLF. Kiiza and his small unit were herded together and ordered to climb into a long, shallow trench, where they lay down side by side, their faces pressed against the cold red ground. The commander of the UNLF soldiers then began shooting the Ugandans with his pistol, one by one, as they writhed in the pit, screaming. Mid-way through the slaughter, the commander ran out of bullets.

"God was sparing me," said Kiiza.

Kiiza was imprisoned in Dar es Salaam, the Tanzanian capital. To torture him, his jailers mixed sand with his *posho*—the Ugandan staple of boiled, mashed cassava—which caused him terrible gastrointestinal pain. He shat blood. "The Red Cross visited me and they were taking many pictures," he said. But nothing came of this visit. Eventually Kiiza stopped eating his *posho*.

When the fighting ended in 1980, Kiiza and the remainder of his unit were repatriated to Uganda. By this time, however, Amin's predecessor Milton Obote had regained power after nine years in exile. As a result, Kiiza and other former Amin soldiers were classified as enemies of the state. So he was imprisoned in his own country, in Jinja, a town on Lake Victoria at the traditional Source of the Nile. After one year, Kiiza so missed his family that he decided to escape, and one night, using old clothes tied together, he lowered himself out of a broken window. He paid a fisherman to ferry him across the lake and hid in the bush for two days.

When he finally arrived at his village, a few kilometers from the Kenyan border, he learned that the Ugandan military had reached his home ahead of him and had killed his wife and his children using machetes. The village women informed him that his wife had been raped before her murder. Kiiza retreated into the bush, fearful that the soldiers would discover him. Crossing the Kenyan border at Malaba, where the East African Railway slices through the bush on its long trip from the Indian Ocean, he took refuge in a small Catholic mission. From there he walked one hundred fifty miles southeast to Nairobi.

In Nairobi, Kiiza was able to start a *duka*, a small general store that stocked inexpensive goods. Eventually he married a Ugandan woman who bore him three children, and he began to eke out a living. Still, he said, he worried about the Ugandan authorities. One day, while he was walking in downtown Nairobi, a Kenyan police car approached him. Three policemen jumped out of the car, grabbed him, beat him, and threw him into the trunk of the car. (Kiiza speculated that the Ugandan government had conspired with the Kenyan police to effect his abduction.)

It was stifling in the trunk; the only air came through cracks where the metal had rusted through. Every half hour or so, the police would stop the car, open the trunk, and beat Kiiza with their fists as he lay in the trunk. They stripped him of his clothes, tossing them onto the road.

After a few hours, from the feel of the bumpy road and the smell of the dirt, Kiiza determined that they had left Nairobi. His only chance, he realized, was to spring open the trunk, which he did by repeatedly kicking at the lock. Finally, the trunk flew open and Kiiza jumped out, falling onto the dirt road. He found himself in the National Game Reserve at Lake Nakuru, fifty kilometers north of Nairobi, where, he realized, the police were planning to execute him and leave him for the animals. Kiiza heard the car stop and the police pursuing him. Panicked, he ran through the bush, the sharp thorns tearing at his skin. In desperation he knelt down, naked and barefoot. He cried aloud, "Help me, God! I have nothing!"

After a few hours of eluding his captors, Kiiza made his way out of the game reserve to a petrol station and hitched a ride back to Nairobi, where he found his family hiding in his store. From other Ugandan refugees in Nairobi he learned that JRS might be able to help him with his business.

When I met Kiiza he was determined to provide for his family. Our office helped him with his modest *duka*, where he sold toilet paper, Malariquine pills, matches, candy, soap, and Fanta soda. He did quite well.

I HAD HIGH HOPES for each of the refugee businesses we sponsored. At the start of every new project, I envisioned the refugees eagerly toiling away at their businesses, efficiently earning enough funds for food and rent. But my somewhat Western expectations often proved meaningless. Life in Africa threw up obstacles before even the most conscientious, making "business as usual" unusual. Still, the refugees' dogged persistence astounded me. The invariable response when they were asked how business was going was "*Tunaendelea, pole pole.*" Or, "We are pushing on, Brother, slowly slowly."

Occurrences that would undoubtedly halt Americans in their tracks were expected and accepted in Africa. "Business is slow, Brother," confessed Jane Tusiime, the Ugandan woman who embroidered animal designs onto barkcloth. "My landlord has thrown me out of my house, and now I am living on the street with my children."

"Somehow I am just a bit sick today," an Ethiopian man said between hacking coughs. "I am having tuberculosis."

The refugees had, in fact, developed an existential worldview that was eminently reasonable under the circumstances. It was a strange amalgam of diligence and acquisitiveness. They had learned the first part of this ethos in their native countries: hard work meant success, whether in the home, on the farm, or in business.

The second part, which could fairly be summed up as "get while the getting is good," was a lesson learned during their long sojourns in the camps. You never knew if "it"—food, clothing, any form of material assistance—would ever be available again.

We gave Loyce Adupa, a Ugandan woman, an electric sewing machine—the reliable Singer 241N—after she explained how much she could use it in her business. The Chinese-made machine she used to mend clothes was forever breaking down, and repairs were more than she could afford.

A few weeks after she had received her new machine, we drove to her place in a rural village outside of Nairobi, called Gachie. Loyce, a mother of three children, belonged to one of the many Christian sects in town; as a symbol of her religious affiliation she wore a white cotton scarf around her head. Loyce led me into her small wooden shack and asked me to sit down. A meal of roasted peanuts and beef stew was placed before me. At this point I was still nervous about eating food prepared by the refugees, for fear of food poisoning or hepatitis, two common enough illnesses in Kenya. But I had decided always to accept food that was prepared by refugees, or friends, or people with whom I worked since it was part of my job. On the other hand, I knew that I didn't want to eat too much; the beef stew had probably cost Loyce a few days' earnings. If I could eat sparingly, I could show that I enjoyed her food and enable her to save some for herself and her children.

During our meal, I noticed that her new Singer Model 241N sat in its unopened box in the middle of her unlit wooden shack. In the middle of the dark room, however, sat an inexpensive Chinese-made machine surrounded by scraps of fabric.

"Loyce," I asked, "Why aren't you using your new machine?"

"But there is no electricity, Brother."

Initially, I was too surprised to say anything. I was finally able to ask the logical question as politely as I could. "Then why did you ask for an electric machine?"

Loyce explained patiently that while she did not have electricity now, perhaps *someday* she would get electricity, and besides, when would she ever get the opportunity for another electric sewing machine? It was hard to disagree with her logic.

Above all, I wanted to guard against too much short-term thinking, of which the most unfortunate example was a refugee selling a piece of JRS-donated equipment for emergency funds. It was tempting, of course, but I felt it needed to be avoided at all costs. So when Specie Kantegwa, a Rwandese mother, confessed that she had sold her sewing machine, I became indignant.

Didn't she see how shortsighted that was? That she had given up her chance for future earnings?

"It was very foolish," I said.

Specie listened patiently to my harangue, and, after I had finished, she explained why she had sold her machine.

Specie was a taciturn woman whose most distinguishing feature was two prominent front teeth separated by a wide space. She entered my office carrying a child wrapped in a red and orange *khanga* cloth knotted at Specie's neck and waist. She swiftly loosened the ties, shifted the baby from her back to her front in one motion, and sat down. Unbuttoning her blouse, she began nursing her baby. With a lisp, she told me how to pronounce her first name: "spacy." Last year she and her sister had been awarded a project. Together, they worked out of Specie's flat sewing dresses in the Central African style—with boldly patterned fabrics and embroidered necklines.

Like many Rwandese refugees, Specie had migrated to Kenya with her parents in the mid-1970s. In 1973, the Rwandese government initiated a program drastically limiting Tutsi opportunity in the country; at the same time, Hutu gangs began their attacks on schools in Rwanda, in an effort to drive out Tutsi students. As a result, thousands of Tutsis, including Specie and her family, fled the country. Like other refugees, the Rwandese were unable to raise sufficient funds for the return trip home. (Many, not surprisingly, did not want to return home, out of fear.) So the Rwandese remained in Nairobi—in a permanent state of flux. For no matter how long they had resided in Kenya, the Kenyan government still classified them (and their children) as refugees.

Now, a new wave of refugees fleeing the recent genocide in Rwanda streamed into Kenya. According to tradition, the Rwandese in Nairobi opened their homes to their compatriots. Though Specie already lived with her sister and her sister's daughter, she accommodated five newly arrived relatives in her cramped flat.

Living in Specie's slum neighborhood were also many poor Kenyans. One of her neighbors retained a Maasai man who acted as an *askari* while the neighbor was at work. "This Maasai," said Specie, "was *mkali sana.*" Very fierce. One day, Specie's niece climbed a tree while holding a plastic cup of water. She accidentally dropped the cup, which landed on the head of the *askari*. Everyone laughed at the Maasai. Enraged by the laughter, he pulled Specie's niece from the tree and began to beat her.

The neighbors ran to Specie's sister. "Your daughter is being beaten!" they said. She wept when she repeated this part of the story. Specie's sister ran over and struggled to pull the man away from her daughter. As she did so, the Maasai reached into his jacket, pulled out a kitchen knife, and slit the throat of Specie's sister. She bled to death in front of her daughter.

As a result, Specie was left to care for her orphaned niece and found herself with no money to buy food for the girl.

I knew instantly that I had been wrong to judge Specie. And, as would happen over and over during my time in Nairobi, I realized that, faced with her situation, I would have made precisely the same choice. Sell the sewing machine and risk the possible annoyance of Brother Jim in order to feed a child? Or keep the sewing machine, and keep Brother Jim happy, but have your niece go without food? It was not a difficult decision.

After Specie finished her story she lifted her face from her nursing child and turned toward me. "Now, Brother," she said calmly. "That is why I sold my machine. May I have a new Singer so I can be starting over?"

THE POSSESSION OF DOCUMENTS from the UN High Commissioner of Refugees (attesting to the legality of a refugee's presence in a country) failed to prevent the Kenyan police from harassing, jailing, beating, and, most frequently, extorting bribes from refugees. The Kenyan government did little to discourage this. A few months after my arrival in Kenya, President Daniel arap Moi issued a series of public statements deriding refugees in Nairobi—particularly the Ugandans—as car thieves. In point of fact, much of the burgling was done by the Kenyan police. A Danish friend of mine had once emerged from a store in Nairobi to see her car being driven away. She chased the car on foot through town to Government House, where the car stopped and two policemen emerged, laughing.

A Sudanese man named John Christian arrived at our office one afternoon from the Lokichoggio camp near the Sudanese border. John, a tall man with bloodshot eyes, was twenty-five. One of his cousins was already enrolled in Sister Luise's scholarship program. John painted highly detailed, brilliantly colored watercolor portraits of Sudanese men and women. We would later sponsor his business by purchasing paint, brushes, and paper for him. On his first visit John brought along a friend to translate his Acholi into English. At one point he described his arrest at the hands of the Kenyan police.

John patiently related his story through the translator. The police had taken John's UN papers and torn them up. John's head sank, and he wept, tears tracing dark lines on his dry skin. This was about the worst fate that could befall a refugee in Nairobi. It guaranteed that, sooner or later, the refugee would be thrown into jail.

To torture him at the police station, the officers had shot off a pistol with the barrel held close to his head, John said.

The translator paused, "But now he is ... ah ... what is the word?" He held out his hands, palms up. I called in Virginia, our cleaning lady, a Kenyan, for help.

"*Kiziwi*," said the translator in Swahili.

"Deaf," said Virginia. "This word means deaf."

I had quite forgotten about Khadija Nakyobe's promise, until she brought her newborn son to the Mikono Centre.

KHADIJA'S SON

At the very dawn of creation
your Spirit breathed on the waters
making them the wellspring of Holiness.
—From *The Roman Missal*: Easter Vigil,
The Blessing of the Water

Khadija Nakyobe made brilliantly colored floor mats fashioned out of braided, dyed straw: from huge, room-sized mats to tiny table mats, in any style or shape. Nearly every week Khadija visited us at Mikono Centre, carrying the heavy mats wrapped in an old sheet slung over her back. When she untied the sheet the mats would roll onto our scuffed parquet floor in a river of color: one pink, emerald green, and yellow, another a deep violet and beige, another carmine red and orange. She was extremely talented, and her mats were popular with both Kenyan and expat customers.

Khadija was an affable young Ugandan woman with three young children. On her first visit she bore a letter. Like many of the refugees, she dictated her thoughts to a literate friend—in essence, a scribe. These letters of introduction typically began with a flowery greeting, reminiscent of the letters of St. Paul.

"Dear Brother Jim," it would read, "I greet you in the name of our Lord Jesus Christ...." The introduction was invariable. Then a variation of: "... who is blessing me by sending you in His name. We are always thanking God for you, who is being very kind to all of us." Finally: "Brother, I greet you and your family. How are they? Please be sending them my greetings." And so on for a full page.

On the opposite side would come the request: a business project, medical assistance, money for food, for baby clothes, for sewing machine repairs, for a child's school fees, for rent.

Khadija's request was for a project to enable her, along with two other Ugandan women, to produce more mats—a proposal Uta and I happily approved.

One day Khadija announced she was pregnant. This was something of a surprise, since I hadn't known that she was married. But by then I knew better than to ask too many questions.

"Brother," she said smiling, "if this baby is a boy, I will be naming him James Martin. If it is a girl the name will be Uta."

I was very honored, I said, though the idea of an African child running around with those names was difficult to imagine. "James Martin" was bad enough, but "Uta" ...

Khadija didn't appear for a couple of months. She was, as the refugees would say, "lost!" One day, though, she appeared in my office with an infant. I had forgotten about her promise.

"This is James Martin!" she said laughing, and handed her child to me. I cradled him in my arms and stared at his unblinking brown eyes.

"Do you think that I should get Jimmy baptized?" Khadija asked.

Now, I certainly was not the kind of missionary that went about forcibly "converting" people. Catholic missionaries had, more or less, given up such overly aggressive practices of conversion years ago. On the other hand, I certainly wasn't going to *prevent* someone from getting baptized. After all, one aspect of being a Christian is inviting new members into your faith. So I agreed that Jimmy should be baptized.

"But we are Muslim," said Khadija.

Huh?

"Yes, I am a Muslim. Should I have Jimmy baptized?"

This was trickier, at least theologically, as I had no experience with this sort of thing. Would I be forcing Khadija to renounce her faith—simply on my recommendation? This seemed ill advised, so I decided a better approach would simply be to remind her that baptism was a major decision for one's child. Though I was happy that she wanted Jimmy to be a Christian, she shouldn't baptize him simply to make me happy. And if she was planning to have Jimmy baptized, she needed to know a little more about Christianity, herself. Perhaps, I suggested, she could visit her local Catholic parish, where she could receive some instruction.

A few weeks later, she again appeared at my office. "I am *very* happy!" she said. The baptism of James Martin, she explained with a broad smile, would happen on Sunday. Would I be the godfather?

Sure, I said, but what about you? What did you decide for yourself?

"Oh, I am already baptized!" she answered. "My Christian name is now Elizabeth. In the Bible, this is the name of Mary's cousin."

But all of this, she continued, meant that little Jimmy needed some baptismal clothes, for which I dutifully provided her five hundred shillings. On Sunday, I held Jimmy once again, this time over a baptismal font, and I watched the parish priest pour water over his head and welcome James Martin into the Christian community. Afterwards, my Jesuit community hosted Elizabeth, Jimmy, and the rest of her family for Fantas and biscuits.

A few weeks later, another Ugandan woman brought her baby boy to see me. "This is James Martin," said Irene Mukasa.

I was delighted. But Alice Nabwire, my shrewd Ugandan friend, saw it otherwise.

I should not have given Khadija those baptism clothes, Alice said one afternoon in my office after I had finished buying some tie-dyed material from her. She shook her head in a way that suggested the matter was beyond consideration.

I was puzzled. Why not?

"Now, Brother," she began slowly, as if she were talking to an idiot or a particularly dense child. "If Khadija and Irene are naming their babies James Martin, and if you are giving Khadija and Irene money for these baby clothes, then surely Brother, aren't you seeing that soon there will be many, many babies in Nairobi called James Martin?"

In Malindi

There is nothing more to tell you except that we are about to embark. We close by asking Christ our Lord for the grace of seeing each other joined together in the next life; for I do not know if we shall ever see each other again in this, because of the great distance between Rome and India and the great harvest to be found. . . .

—St. Francis Xavier, in a letter
to St. Ignatius Loyola,
from Lisbon, Portugal,
March 18, 1541

After a year in Nairobi I decided I needed a vacation. So, along with three other Jesuits, I took a trip to Mombasa, the Kenyan port that lies on the Indian Ocean. We made reservations at a retreat house, run by the Italian Consolata Fathers, that was reputed to have the best Italian food in East Africa.

The eight-hour trip was scenic, if uncomfortable. To reach the coast from Nairobi one travels on the Mombasa Road through the Tsavo region—a dry, flat area of tall savanna grasses, dotted with colossal baobab trees and low thorn bushes, among which move zebras, elands, giraffes, ostriches, and Thomson's gazelles (known locally as "Tommys"). It was extremely hot. The road itself is somewhat dangerous, owing to a considerable number of giraffes that lope across the road, oblivious to cars or *matatus*. As a Kenyan friend told me before my trip, if a *matatu* is unlucky enough to run into a giraffe, "The giraffe will win."

In the early part of this century, Tsavo gained international notoriety as the spot where the building of the East African Railway was halted, owing to some difficulties with the local wildlife. The story, wildly improbable but true, is featured in a number of books, most recently Charles Miller's *The Lunatic Express*, the frankly incredible tale of the building of the Railway. The Railway crosses not only Tsavo, but the Rift Valley, the Nile and, not incidentally, thousands of kilometers of rocky mountains and scorching deserts. A few hundred kilometers inland, two enormous lions—the "Man-Eaters of Tsavo"—terrorized the Kenyan and Indian workers whom the British had brought in for the job, completely shutting down the Progress of Empire. (The story would serve as the basis for the 1997 movie *The Ghost and the Darkness*.)

For months the two lions snatched men from the work camps, mostly at night, but often in broad daylight. Nothing could stop them: neither guards posted in the trees (they ate them), nor *boma* fences made of tall thorn bushes (supposed to have been "lion-proof," the man-eaters got through them anyway), nor most famously, a man-made trap. A railway car was fashioned to afford a marksman seated inside (behind a row of metal bars) the ability to shoot any lion that drew near. On its first night of use one of the lions simply climbed through a back window and dragged the man away, leaving behind only the marksman's rifle and a trail of gore.

After months of terror Colonel J.H. Patterson, the intrepid leader of the Crown's mission, finally brought down the two lions in a harrowing hunt. These exploits formed the basis of his own ripping yarn entitled—what else?—*The Man-Eaters of Tsavo.*

My own experiences with lions—outside of viewing them in the game reserve from the relative safety of my jeep—were limited to stories. A Tanzanian Jesuit related the tale of sleeping in a Jesuit community in Zambia. The community was, like many religious houses in temperate zones, arranged around a courtyard opening onto a broad lawn. After a refreshing shower one evening, the Jesuit returned to his room and, before retiring, sprinkled himself with talcum powder. The next morning he noticed on the floor a pair of large lion tracks, clearly marked in the white powder, that entered the room, stopped at the bedside, and then exited.

"*Simba,*" remarked the Jesuit dryly, "decided not to eat me."

Joseph, the Maasai watchman at our community in Nairobi, a young man of nineteen, told me how all Maasai boys must kill a lion before becoming a *moran*, or warrior. He had already done so, he said proudly. I asked him how—expecting a long description of the hunt: the tradition, the planning, the execution.

Instead, Joseph simply crouched low, raised a closed right hand back to his shoulder, as if carrying a spear. "*Kama hivi!*" he said. Like this. He made a quick thrusting motion and a whistling sound with his teeth.

Another Maasai friend related his boyhood experiences as a shepherd. One day, leaning wearily on his shepherd's staff, he noticed, in his words, "These sheep were jumping into the air." Finding this unusual, he approached his flock and saw among the sheep what he thought was a very large dog. He beat it with his stick until it ran away. "But he was no dog," said my friend. "He was *simba.*" My friend said that if he had been older he would surely have known better.

And more recently, the Jesuit retreat house, whose land abuts the Nairobi Game Reserve, had run into some problems with *simba*. The Kenyan cook appeared one night at dinner, shaken, and announced, "I am hearing *simba*." The following day a Jesuit priest spotted lion tracks on the grounds of the retreat house.

Retreatants were advised not to venture out at dusk or dawn (*simba*'s preferred mealtime) and to stay close to the house in general. When I made my retreat there, I did the same, despite the addition of a new fence around the property. The Jesuits assured me it was "lion-proof"—the same words, I noted, used at Tsavo.

WE ARRIVED AT THE RETREAT HOUSE in Mombasa at three in the afternoon and a cheerful, fat Italian priest with a shiny, bald head led us to our quarters. He escorted me through the grounds of the villa to a spacious room that opened directly onto the beach. Next to the doorway lime-green lizards sunned themselves on a concrete patio lit white by the equatorial sun. Palm trees swayed slowly in the humid breeze before the Indian Ocean. On the horizon could be seen grey American warships, gravely making their way up the coast to Somalia.

An overhead fan blew noiselessly in the room. "You are most welcome to this villa, Father." Thanks, I said, but told him that I was not yet a priest.

"You're not?" he sniffed. "Well then, come this way." He picked up my bag and walked out of the room. I followed, confused. He led me behind the other rooms to a small, dark room with one window that faced the parking lot. "The other rooms are for the *fathers*," he said pointedly.

ONE OF THE REASONS for my trip to the coast was a desire to see Malindi, a town a few kilometers north of Mombasa. Malindi is a favorite spot for adventurous European travelers and a particular magnet for Italians. Approaching the town one passes signs for *Chiesa Cattolica* and Italian advertisements for real estate. But apart from the beach and a few Italian restaurants there is little that is remarkable in Malindi. There is, however, sitting on a peninsula on the ocean, a gilt cross perched atop a lonely stone cairn that faces toward India. The cairn is more modern, but the cross was erected in the fifteenth century by Vasco da Gama to help ships navigate their way up the coast.

One of the first things we saw, as we navigated our own way around the town, was Vasco da Gama's cross. Another Jesuit who saw this cross, four hundred fifty years earlier, was the great missionary St. Francis Xavier on his way to "the Indies." In a letter to his Jesuit brothers in Rome, dated the 20th of September, 1542, he wrote:

> *It took us more than two months to sail from Mozambique to Goa. On our way we passed Melinde, a city of peaceful Moors. . . . The Christians who die there are buried in large tombs adorned with crosses. Near the city the Portuguese have erected a large stone cross that is gilded and very beautiful. God our Lord knows how much consolation we received from the sight of it, knowing its great efficacy and seeing it there so alone and so victorious.*

The reason for our visit was a small chapel within sight of the cross. Here Francis Xavier celebrated Mass during his brief stay in Kenya. The chapel sits framed by coconut palm trees beside the cerulean Indian Ocean. It is a perfectly square building with whitewashed stucco walls crowned by a high pointed roof of thatched brown grass. The roof is topped with a simple wooden cross. A small graveyard surrounds the chapel, and somewhere among the graves of Catholic Kenyans and an English baronet lies a friend of Francis who died en route to Malindi.

> *In Melinde I buried a man who had died on our galleon. The Moors were edified on seeing how we Christians conduct ourselves when we bury our dead.*

Inside we saw what Francis probably saw: a dirt floor and a bare stone altar. On the day of our visit, however, on the altar rested a small prayer card wrapped in cellophane held together with yellowing tape. In another corner someone had left a pious picture of St. Anthony holding the infant Jesus. Sacks of cement and a workman's cast-off sneakers sat in a corner.

> *One of the most distinguished Moors of this city of Melinde
> asked me to tell him whether the churches in which we are
> accustomed to pray are much frequented by us, and
> whether we are fervent in prayer, since, as he told me, they
> themselves had lost a great deal of their devotion, and he
> wished to know if the same had happened among
> Christians.*

In 1991, as part of the Ignatian Year celebrations—the five
hundredth anniversary of the birth of St. Ignatius—the Jesuits of
East Africa refurbished the chapel. The small, green, wooden
sign outside recounting the history of the site was new. One of
the Jesuits explained that the sign was designed to be unobtru-
sive for fear of possibly offending the largely Muslim population.
A different attitude than that of Xavier who, in responding to
the Moor's questions, reported:

> *He was not satisfied with what I told him, that God our
> Lord, being most faithful in all his works, is not pleased
> with infidels and still less with their prayers; and this was
> the reason why God wanted their prayers to cease, for he
> was not pleased with them.*

But the small sign was sensible, considering the predominance of Islam here. In fact, when we arrived we were cheerfully
greeted by the chapel's caretaker—a young Muslim boy.

Three of us celebrated Mass in the dim chapel—an
American scholastic working with refugees, a Maltese priest
working in the novitiate in Tanzania, and the Rwandese priest
who ran the theologate in Nairobi. The young caretaker politely
swept the altar with an evergreen branch and silently brought us
two sprigs of magenta bougainvillea for the altar. We placed a
newspaper on the dusty altar to keep the linens clean. And from
under the altar linens a headline from the Nairobi *Daily Nation*
peered out: "Man, 70, Rapes Girl." Outside a chicken clucked,
and we could hear music drifting on the sea breeze.

During the Mass I thought about Francis Xavier. What was it like for him in Malindi? In a time of planes and phones and faxes could I really appreciate what it meant for Xavier to be so far from home, unaware of what was happening with his companions in Europe except from months-old letters?

How could I understand someone like Francis Xavier? Here was a person who, without blanching, could write:

A very learned Moor of the sect of Mohammed . . . was living in the city. He told me that if Mohammed did not come to visit them within two years, he would no longer believe in him or his sect. It is only fitting that infidels and great sinners should live in diffidence.

Arrogant? Perhaps. But this was the same man who worked tirelessly among unfamiliar peoples, devoting his life to bringing them what he considered to be the good news. And this same Francis could express gratitude later on when he encountered a group of indigenous people on the island of Socotra who shared with him what little food they had:

Out of their poverty, with much affection and good will, they gave me what they had.

As I stood in St. Francis' chapel, I knew that I probably could understand very little about the mindset of a sixteenth-century saint, at least from the perspective of twentieth-century Catholicism. I doubt, for example, that Francis Xavier would have had much trouble with the question: "Should Khadija Nakyobe have her son baptized?" In his day, the prevailing idea among missionaries was to baptize everybody, and let God sort it out.

Still, I realized in the chapel that I might be able to learn from the faith of someone who, despite separation from his companions, the strangeness of a totally foreign culture, and a decidedly medieval perspective still struggled to find God where he was and in the people he called "infidels."

Agostino Alikutepa, a refugee from Mozambique, was a skilled woodcarver who learned his craft from a fellow Mozambiquan, an elderly man named Zechariah. Agostino's expertise was a source of constant amazement for me. So was his faith.

THE TREE OF LIFE

Did God not choose those who are poor in the
world to be rich in faith, and heirs to the kingdom
that he promised to those who love him?
—*The Letter of James 2:5*

In addition to officially sponsored projects, Uta and I helped refugees who did not, for one reason or another, qualify for assistance but who were already making things on their own.

Many refugees put to use the traditional skills they had learned in their home countries. Ethiopian men fashioned purses, belts, and small crosses from leather. Ugandan women wove floor mats and baskets from straw. Mozambiquan men carved ebony sculptures. Rwandese women traditionally spent up to six months inside their houses following their weddings, weaving geometrically patterned baskets out of sisal. These were used at home and as gifts for relatives. Gauddy brought these baskets to us regularly; they sold briskly at the American embassy bazaars.

AGOSTINO ALIKUTEPA was one of the Mozambiquan wood carvers. He worked with another Mozambiquan, an older man named Zechariah, carving ebony statues. Each month the two made the long bus trip to Mombasa where they purchased the expensive rosewood necessary for their carvings. If they were able they would also buy *mpingo* logs, a honey-colored wood with a black center—ebony.

There were, of course, hundreds of Kenyan and Tanzanian carvers working in Nairobi, catering to a thriving tourist trade. They turned out all types of carvings—animals, animal heads, spoons and forks with animal heads, Maasai warriors, African busts, and the like. Even poorly made goods sold briskly.

When I first met Agostino he was carrying a large burlap sack containing some samples of his work. He looked like some of the other Mozambiquans I knew, with a round, almost plump, face and liquid brown eyes. I asked whether he made anything like what I had seen in the city markets. He looked offended and averred that he would never sell such low-quality goods.

"Zechariah has been carving since he was small," he said. "Now he has taken me on as his apprentice." From his bag he produced smooth ebony busts topped with intricate hair styles, animals made from aromatic rosewood polished to a mirror-like shine, and a large head of Christ, whose gleaming dark face receded into the rough *mpingo* bark. The quality was indeed higher than that of the city markets. I asked Zechariah and Agostino if they might consider sitting outside our shop and carving. Perhaps this would help their business by exposing them to new customers. As an incentive I offered them new carving tools. They agreed.

It was an unqualified success. Tourists made a beeline to the two men working underneath an enormous ficus tree in our front yard, surrounded by white, brown and black wood shavings. Often I purchased the finished work for sale in our shop. But sometimes visitors spied a work in progress and reserved it, returning to pick it up after it was completed. The two men were ecstatic.

Agostino and Zechariah also kept a stock of finished goods at home which they brought in from time to time. One afternoon, they asked me to join them under the ficus tree, where a burlap bag covered what looked like a small black log. They removed the covering to reveal a three-foot-high ebony sculpture of twisting forms. On closer inspection I saw it was groupings of dozens of men and women holding hands, working in a garden, nursing children, kissing, dancing, and climbing up the trunk. It was fantastic—unlike anything I had seen before.

"This is the Tree of Life," Zechariah explained. "It is part of our tradition." It had taken three months to carve.

Unfortunately, it was far too expensive. Their asking price was 35,000 shillings—roughly $500 US. I reminded him that our customers preferred smaller items to carry home with them overseas or small decorations for their houses in Nairobi. Larger, more expensive items like their sculpture would not sell.

"But this *mpingo* is very beautiful," Agostino said confidently. "Surely, this will sell."

Well, I doubt that, I said. Even if it would sell, the shop could not afford to buy something like that. Our budget wouldn't allow it.

Perhaps, replied Agostino, you could place it in the shop without paying for it. If someone likes it they could buy it. Somewhat embarrassed that, despite my Wharton education, Agostino had a more fluid business mind than I did, I told him that sounded fine. This is called consignment, I said.

"And you will pray that it sells, Brother?" he asked.

Sure.

Together we carried the heavy piece of wood into the shop. It weighed at least fifty pounds. Three Ugandan women waiting to see me hurried to admire the carving and ran their fingers over the intertwined people making their way up the tall stump. They used a common East African expression of approval—a short, aspirated, "Ah!"—over and over.

Five minutes later I heard the crunch of a car pulling up on the gravel path outside. An English tourist stepped from a forest green Land Rover and entered the shop. We chatted for a few minutes, and her eye alighted on the Tree of Life. "This is exquisite," she announced and asked about its provenance. I called in Agostino to explain how he had carved it and the significance of the human figures. She bought it for 45,000 shillings.

"Ah, Brother, you see?," Agostino whispered as the woman's car pulled away. "Your prayers were answered."

CONSOLATION

> If a man leaves his dreamy conceptions aside and focuses on his naked poverty, when the masks fall and the core of his being is revealed, it soon becomes obvious that he is religious by nature. In the midst of his existence there unfolds the bond (re-ligio) which ties him to the infinitely transcendent mystery of God, the insatiable interest in the absolute that captivates him and underlines his poverty.
>
> —Johannes B. Metz, *Poverty of Spirit*

After the Mikono Centre had been open for some time, I settled into something resembling a routine. Wake at 6 A.M., thanks to either the dazzling equatorial sunlight that streamed into my room or to a reliable pair of Egyptian ibises who flew over the house at precisely that hour, cawing loudly. Roll over and switch on a shortwave radio that a forgetful American visitor had left behind and listen to the BBC World Service. Shower (when there was enough hot water), pray (when I was good enough to remember it), breakfast (tea and a banana) with my Jesuit housemates, glance at the *Daily Nation,* and then drive through Kawangware on the way to Kangemi (if the jeep was working). Usually I'd spot refugees in the slums on their way to visit me; I'd pick them up and we'd start our meeting in the jeep. If I didn't see them, they'd always see me. One day a refugee darted out in front of my jeep. I slammed on the brakes, screeched dramatically, swerved crazily, and barely avoided hitting him. He leaned into the car. "Brother, you are worse than these *matatus!*"

When I arrived at Mikono Centre, the sun already blazing in the clear sky, there were normally a dozen or so refugees waiting for me on the shady porch, mostly women, some nursing children, many bearing crafts they had carried that morning on the *matatu,* others holding letters requesting a small business grant. "*Jambo,* Brother!"

Most of the morning was spent meeting with the refugees. Some needed advice on their projects—keeping the books, dealing with landlords and merchants, resolving arguments, finding new markets—and most requested some financial assistance to help them through a rough time. I met with the refugees in a small room furnished with simple wooden chairs and a low table, where we could talk freely, sometimes in English, sometimes in Swahili, sometimes in French. If a refugee spoke a language that I didn't know, say, Arabic or Luganda or Portuguese, there was usually another refugee willing to translate. In this way, I felt as if we were all working together toward a common goal.

The time we spent together, I soon realized, was one of the most important things I could give the refugees. All of them had been for much of their lives forced to wait and wait and wait in endless lines—in the camps, in the UN offices, in government offices, in jails, in hospitals. And when in those places they were finally ushered in to see this or that official, they were typically treated shabbily and dealt with as quickly as possible. So I was happy to sit with them and listen as carefully as I could to their concerns. Time, not just money, was something that I could easily give them, and it cost nothing.

Most refugees brought goods they hoped to sell and, like Alice Nabwire, would make a good case for why, if I wanted two, I should buy three instead. Already the shop was doing well financially, so it was easy to accommodate most such requests. Besides, even if we ended up buying too much merchandise, the money was going to a good cause. Better to have an overflow of baskets on our shelves than to allow a family to go hungry.

Often, though, we were visited by refugees who simply wanted money—a more difficult situation. Though the purpose of our work was to help the refugees support themselves, there were still many in need of immediate assistance, mainly to buy food. Usually, I steered them to their local parishes, where JRS had started a program of providing cash assistance for the emergency needs of refugees throughout Nairobi. But some needed money immediately. One day a Sudanese woman, carrying a child on her back, sat down in my office and begged for "some little money." She had no money for "school fees." The Kenyan public schools were officially free but demanded exorbitant school fees for spurious projects, such as building funds for buildings that never materialized. What's more, she said, her children had no food.

When I told her she would need to visit her local parish, she burst into tears. She had, she said, not even enough money for bus fare. She cried and cried and dried her eyes on her skirt. "Oh, Brother," she said over and over. Finally I gave her money of my own. Of course, when she emerged onto the porch her face told the other refugees that I had given her what she asked for. (It was also, I discovered, easy for them to hear what was going on through the open windows.) One Rwandese refugee reminded me of my breach of procedure. "Brother, you should not give *money* out," he scolded. "You should be sending her to the parish!"

In between visits from the refugees, I would assist customers who frequented our shop, showing off our wares and explaining the mission of JRS. Often, even the briefest descriptions of the lives of the refugees impelled customers to purchase a good deal more than they had intended to. And I was not above using the occasional measure of guilt to encourage larger purchases. One day I noticed an American woman examining a barkcloth bag made by Jane Tusiime, upon which was embroidered a smiling zebra.

"Could a child use this as a bookbag?" asked our customer as she fingered the rough barkcloth.

"Sure," I replied, having never considered the possibility.

"And would it stand up to rain, do you think?"

"I guess so," I offered lamely, desperately trying to figure that out. "I mean it's bark, right? Trees do pretty well in the rain."

She laughed. "You'd say just about anything to sell these, wouldn't you?"

"Well," I said, "they're wonderful bags, and pretty sturdy ... but yes, I probably *would* say anything. The woman who makes these is going through a rough time right now. She's just been kicked out of her house." Not surprisingly, the woman bought three. And somewhere in the States is a young boy dragging his books to school in a wet barkcloth bag.

In the afternoon, I visited the refugees in the slums. Some of them were unable to visit Mikono Centre due to their work; on other occasions I wanted to check up on them, to see how well they were working together and if I could offer any advice. Usually, I would be asked to adjudicate a dispute, talk to a truculent landlord, or investigate a broken machine. And so my afternoons usually consisted of long drives through the hot city to discover a woman sitting forlornly in a fish-and-chips stand, where she would shake her head and tell me how very slow business was. Or to a woman's small home where a new sewing machine sat idle, surrounded by scraps of fabric, for lack of business. On these occasions, I would sit with them and simply listen to their frustrations and their problems. For my part, I tried to listen carefully and then offer whatever practical advice I could.

At times I felt overwhelmed by the poverty and misery and sickness that they faced—the seeming lack of hope, the enormity of their problems. But seeing refugee after refugee helped me to feel that I was helping out, even if in a small way. Happily, I quickly rid myself of the idea that I would be able to solve *all* of their problems, as a sort of refugee savior. Ironically, this realization was rather easy to come to, thanks to working in Nairobi. Whereas in other locales one might imagine oneself able to do everything, the unpredictable and chaotic situation in Nairobi rendered anyone's notions of omnipotence absurd. This realization, I think, enabled me to relax some about my work. I worked hard but tried to leave the rest to God.

AFTER WORK, I'D DROP OFF the inevitable passenger and return to Loyola House for Mass in our small house chapel. Following Mass, our community, which numbered a dozen or so Jesuits from around the world—Malta, India, Tanzania, Ireland, Belgium, Canada, and the United States—enjoyed some Fantas, peanuts, and beer. At 6 P.M. promptly a bell rang, and we offered grace in our living room. Dinner was consistently simple. The cooks prepared only enough for those who were expected for dinner, and there were rarely extra portions.

The bishop of the diocese of Garissa visited the Jesuit provincial (the regional superior) one evening and lingered in the living room after grace. The rest of the community proceeded to the dining room and filled their plates with chicken marengo, green beans, and potatoes. After a half an hour the bishop and the provincial strolled into the dining room, only to discover the following victuals awaiting them: three string beans and one potato. No one had thought to leave any leftovers. "Ah," the bishop said to general laughter, "the famous Jesuit hospitality."

After dinner came a traditional Jesuit custom: a "visit" to the chapel to pray before the tabernacle housing the Blessed Sacrament, the bread consecrated during the celebration of Mass. When I arrived at Loyola House and discovered this somewhat outmoded practice, I decided immediately that I wouldn't participate. Visiting the Blessed Sacrament, focusing one's piety exclusively on one *thing*, was not something I felt comfortable with. Didn't that box God in, making God available solely as an object? So for the first few weeks of my stay, when the rest of the

Jesuits filed out of the dining room to visit the Blessed Sacrament, I remained behind to clear the plates from the tables.

A few weeks later, the superior of the community asked to see me in his office. Why, he asked gently, was I avoiding the visit after dinner? The priests in the house were wondering why I wasn't participating. Annoyed at even having to explain (wasn't my prayer life *my* business?) I responded simply that this wasn't part of my spirituality. And that, I thought, would be that.

But he suggested that while the visit wasn't part of my spirituality, perhaps it was something I'd like to try. He admitted that it was somewhat outdated, something that younger Jesuits might not appreciate, but could I see my way clear to do it as a way of praying with the community? Grudgingly, I agreed.

The following night after dinner I wandered into the chapel with the rest of the Jesuits. Silently, the men in my community knelt down facing the tabernacle and prayed silently. I knelt, too, resenting every moment of being "forced" to do so. But then, as I looked around the room and saw a dozen men kneeling in prayer together as a community, I was filled with a feeling of quiet, of peace. It was profoundly prayerful. After that I went every night. In the end, I realized that it was not others who were boxing God in: it was me, for refusing to accept the possibility that grace might come to people even in ways that I considered outdated.

Some priests played cribbage after dinner, read the daily papers, perused magazines brought by visitors from the States or Europe, or retired to their rooms to pray. Early on, Jim Corrigan and I discovered a video-rental place in town and hosted video nights for the rest of the community. The videos were obviously pirated and had legends running across the bottom of the screen: "It is forbidden to copy this video," or "For Purposes of the Academy of Motion Picture Arts and Sciences Only. Duplication Forbidden." Which actors were selling their Oscar tapes to Nairobi video pirates? we wondered.

There were two state-owned television networks: KBC,

which broadcast low-budget Swahili dramas and news programs; and KTN, whose fare ran heavily to Australian soap operas, Kenyan cricket matches, and reruns of American shows about African Americans, such as "Roc" and "Family Matters." Friday and Saturday evenings were given over to "Transworld Sports," a British sports program that summarized, on Fridays, every major soccer match in the UK, and on Saturdays, the world. These shows, though interminable, were required viewing in our community.

More entertaining were the Kenyan commercials, which were evenly divided between ads for wonderfully named soaps (British Imperial Leather, Fa, Lady Gay) and insecticides, known locally as *dawa ya wadudu,* or "bug medicine." Marketing, as it turned out, worked on me as well as it did in the States. My choice of bug spray had less to do with its effectiveness, which consisted mostly of drowning the bugs with an overly liberal application, than with its name: Doom.

The evening news in Nairobi began with precisely the same words every night. On KTN: "Today, His Excellency President Daniel arap Moi ..." Then a litany of the president's day. He had opened a chicken hatchery in the Rift Valley. He had visited a secondary school in Mombasa. He had attended Sunday services in Kiambu. He had spoken to the faithful citizens in Eldoret. On KBC one could hear the same, only in Swahili: "*Leo, Mtukufu Rais Daniel arap Moi ...*"

At night I liked a snack of boiled milk with honey. The honey jar, which sat on one of the dining room tables, was filled with the dead ants that invaded the jar. They floated on the top of the honey and were exceedingly difficult to extract. After a few times of making a sticky mess of things, I discovered it was more effective to spoon the honey into a cup of boiling milk, let the ants float to the top, and skim them off. This put me in mind of the old saying that there are three stages to missionary life. In the first stage, you separate the rice from the bugs and eat the rice. After a little while, you simply eat the rice and the bugs together. Finally, you separate the rice from the bugs and eat the bugs. Though I still had a ways to go, perhaps I was, in the words of a seasoned missionary friend, "beginning to arrive."

By ten o'clock, I was in bed reading, after a short period of contemplative prayer, called by Jesuits the *examen*, a sort of review of the day in which one tried to see where God could be found. Often, before falling asleep I would hear one of the older Indian Jesuits at prayer. He walked back and forth in the breeze-way, his sandals shuffling across the terrazzo floor; behind his back he held his rosary, the wooden beads clicking quietly as he walked.

I GREW TO LOVE my work with the refugees and especially enjoyed working in Kangemi. It was the first time I had ever worked in a neighborhood where everyone seemed to know me. (Doubtless my skin color was a big help in that regard.) The refugees I passed on their way to Mikono Centre knew me, to say the least. Greeting them involved a lengthy discussion of their businesses, their health, their families. And then: my business, my health, and—a constant source of surprise no matter how often it happened—my family, a world away in Phila-delphia. "Greet your mother and father for us, Brother!"

The vendors and people selling roasted corn and peanuts along Kangemi's dirt paths knew me as well. I took lunches at St. Joseph the Worker parish and grew friendly with the Jesuits and the staff there. It felt good to be imbedded in the community, particularly in such a poor area of the city. I was happy to be there and happy to be there as a Jesuit.

SOMETIMES MY JEEP was indisposed—either broken down or lent to a car-less friend. On days without my jeep, after work I would walk across to a bus stop, which lay across a deep valley.

One such afternoon, I began the walk home. The long brown path began at the church, St. Joseph the Worker, which perched on a hill overlooking the Kangemi Valley. From there the bumpy path descended through a thicket of floppy-leaved banana trees, tall, green ficus trees, orange day lilies, long, green cowgrass and maize fields. On the way down into the valley I passed people silently working in their *shambas*, their little plots of land, who looked up and called out to me as I passed. Brilliantly colored, iridescent sunbirds—turquoise, violet, and indigo—alighted on the tips of the tall grasses. At the bottom of the valley ran the Nairobi River, little more than a creek except during the rainy season. Groups of old Kikuyu women laughed and joked as they did their families' laundry on the riverbank. The wet clothes were draped on the dusty bushes, where the hot sun dried them quickly.

Spanning the river was a flimsy bridge constructed of sticks and twigs tied together with twine. When the rains came, the little bridge was promptly washed away, and the people in Kangemi simply built another. The first time I used the bridge I walked over it gingerly, prompting one of the women to laugh and offer advice. *"Wewe ni magari sana, Brother! Hakuna shida!"* You are very thin, Brother! Don't worry!

As I climbed the hill away from the river, I paused. Standing on the hardpacked earth, I turned and looked back at St. Joseph the Worker atop the hill. Though it was four in the afternoon, the sun was near its zenith. It blazed down on the valley, illuminating the reddish brown path, the tiny river, the banana trees, the grasses, the people. Quite suddenly I was overwhelmed by joy. I'm happy to be here, I thought, and happy to be working with the refugees. I was exactly where I was supposed to be. I felt useful and fruitful. And I was quite amazed at my happiness, my contentment, my peace.

AFTERWARDS I WONDERED what it was that made me so happy. The day had been an ordinary one, full of the usual daily problems. Nothing particularly exciting had happened, unless you counted a few successful refugee business stories. There were no major dilemmas solved. No refugee's life had been put back together. I hadn't received any particularly good news. My community was the same community it had been for the past two years. I wasn't looking forward to a special trip or holiday. It wasn't a big liturgical feast day. I wasn't planning to see anyone that night for dinner.

St. Ignatius of Loyola, the founder of the Society of Jesus, wrote about what he called "consolation" in the *Spiritual Exercises*, his manual for spiritual directors. He described consolation as an uplifting of the spirit, a feeling that gives comfort and joy. Such consolation, Ignatius wrote in 1541, gives "genuine happiness and spiritual joy, and thereby banishes any sadness or turmoil.... " More precisely, he spoke of "consolation without preceding cause," a feeling that unexpectedly comes over, or passes over, or fills a person quite unexpectedly. This feeling, Ignatius understood from his own experience, was a wonderfully unique gift from God. I've had that type of experience only a few times in my life, but never as intensely as when standing on the hillside that day.

OVER THE BRIDGE, after passing a few small shacks and more *shambas*, I eventually left Kangemi and arrived in Riruta, though neighborhood boundaries were shifting and evanescent. The path continued past a large church in Riruta, St. John the Baptist, the original foundation parish for the later mission parish of St. Joseph the Worker. The Church of St. John the Baptist was more established and looked more like a traditional European church. Like St. Joseph's, the church in Riruta had a large school attached. Drawing closer I passed Kenyan boys and girls in uniform: pale blue blouses and navy skirts for the girls, white shirts (usually torn) and navy pants for the boys. Most went cheerfully barefoot on the dirt path, holding hands.

The bus stop lay just beyond the church. There the old metal bus shelter was grotesquely twisted, the result of an unfortunate meeting with a *matatu*, and sat in a heap by the side of the road. People sat on what would have been its roof. But most just waited in the shade of a large jacaranda tree that stood by the road. The buses came infrequently, and most of the time they were crowded, with people squeezed on, half-in and half-out, desperate to return home. But I never liked to push on, even though passengers would hold their hands out as the bus pulled away, imploring me to grab on for a ride. It wasn't that I minded the discomforts of the trip, I just didn't mind waiting.

Only a few kilometers outside the city, past the green Ngong Hills, one came upon numerous Maasai villages, which dotted the dry landscape. My friend Mark Brown took this picture while staying with a Maasai family in the Kajiado District, south of Nairobi.

SISTER MAUREEN
MAKES AN
UNWISE PURCHASE

Look carefully at what's available before parting
with your money.
    —*Kenya: A Lonely Planet Travel Survival Kit*

For many aid workers in East Africa, Nairobi
was seen as a sort of vacation spot, a concept
I found difficult to understand when our water
ran out, the telephone lines went dead, the electricity failed, the
jeep was immobilized by gooey mud, or I was visited by food
poisoning.

One such visitor was Sister Maureen, one of the many
intrepid Australian sisters who worked with JRS in a refugee
camp in northern Uganda, near a small town called Adjumani.
She had a wonderful sense of humor and a rosy outlook on life,
both of which were put to the test frequently by her work in
Uganda. Not long after her trip to Nairobi, Maureen, two other
sisters, and three Comboni fathers with whom they worked were

abducted from their community in northern Uganda by the Sudanese People's Liberation Army on a trumped-up charge of seditious behavior. These six Catholic missionaries were accused, among other things, of "spreading Islam." After a month in captivity they were released.

One week I drove with Maureen and my Jesuit superior, who was visiting from Boston, into the bush.

It is surprising for the first-time visitor to Nairobi to realize just how close the bush is to the city limits. Within thirty minutes of driving south or southeast one arrives in an arid countryside that looks as if it has sprung directly from the pages of *National Geographic*: broad, lion-colored plains dotted with short thorn bushes; miles of tall savanna grass; vultures wheeling in the sky; herds of zebras and impala resting on the horizon; a warthog family; groups of screaming baboons; the occasional giraffe.

A few kilometers from Loyola House, past the green Ngong Hills, we came to what I called, doubtless incorrectly but for want of a better name, Maasai country. From the road, huddled low in the valley, the Maasai villages could be seen: squat mud huts surrounded by a *boma* of thorn bushes. The Maasai, though still feared in East Africa for their warrior traditions, were essentially a pastoral people. The youngest boys guarded the sheep; the next youngest, the goats; the oldest, cattle. When I once spied a very young Maasai boy chasing a surprisingly swift-footed sheep across a flat field, his plaid *shuka* flapping crazily as he ran, I remembered the passage in the Gospel of Matthew about the good shepherd, who leaves the flock in search of the one lost sheep. If God, I thought, pursues us with anything near the persistence of this young Maasai who now ran headlong across the savanna, then humanity had little to worry about.

The three of us bounced merrily along the road. I pointed out land formations, colossal anthills, animals, and commented on the heat. We noticed a young Maasai woman ahead, selling jewelry. She motioned for us to stop, and we pulled over onto a clearing, raising clouds of red dust.

The woman, her head shorn, clad in the traditional royal blue *shuka* of Maasai women, held out an armful of necklaces as a prodigious number of flies buzzed around her, and then, us. At her feet stood soda bottles filled with fresh honey, the broken combs still floating in the amber liquid.

I asked the price of a necklace. She responded, and, thinking of our prices at Mikono, I rolled my eyes. She laughed, showing us her few teeth.

Sister Maureen spied an unusual necklace on the woman's arm, fashioned out of what looked like brown leaves, which were difficult to identify. "What is it?" I asked Maureen, who was already haggling. She didn't know, she said, and continued her negotiations.

"*Shillingi ngapi?*" Maureen asked. How many shillings?

After Maureen and my Jesuit friend returned to the car, I asked the Maasai woman what the necklace was made of. She told me.

As I depressed the clutch and turned the ignition key, Sister Maureen showed us her new purchase, which she now wore around her neck. She touched the leaves, as the car engine started. "Fifty shillings," she said. "Not bad."

"Yes," I said laughing. "A good price for dried roach wings."

She yelped, and tossed the necklace out the window of the car. Born aloft by dozens of insect wings, it gently floated to the ground.

"Thank you! Thank you!" The Maasai woman shouted in English as we drove away.

ONE THOUSAND GREEN PLASTIC CHRISTMAS CUPS

Akatono kazira mu liiso
You can share even if you have a little.
—Lugandan proverb

After Uta and I had worked together for a year, she was suddenly forced to leave the country. Her husband, Jürgen, had been seriously injured in an accident in Mombasa when a *matatu* had struck his little car. Uta and Jürgen returned to Germany for his recuperation. JRS assigned Michael Schöpf, a young German Jesuit who had recently arrived in Nairobi, to work with me in Uta's place. We both missed Uta, who had contributed enormously to the success of Mikono Centre. So did the refugees, who asked daily now after "Mrs. Uta," as well as "Mr. Uta."

Between the frequent bazaars at the American Embassy and increasing popularity among tourists and religious communities,

A few hours before the Christmas party, I met with Tom Peter Zuze, a sweet-natured Mozambiquan refugee who was an expert craftsman. Like many refugees, Tom had already started a small business for himself even before receiving assistance from us. Here, Tom (on the right) sits on the porch of the Mikono Centre showing off an intricately carved mahogany chair.

the Mikono Centre began to do excellent business. In the first six months, our sales surpassed $50,000 U.S., an astronomical sum in East Africa. We plowed our revenues, of course, into buying more goods from the refugees. There was little overhead, and our salaries—those of Michael and myself, as well as our two Kenyan assistants—were covered by the generous grants that we received from our aid agencies. It was also rather easy to obtain funds from donor agencies, since East Africa—particularly the crisis in Somalia and the U.S. involvement there—were at that time very much in the news. Most of our donors were Catholic relief organizations, though frequently quasi-governmental organizations from western Europe and Japan helped us as well.

As a result, after the first six months of operation, the Mikono Centre found itself with a little surplus money, mostly from unsolicited donations, so Michael and I decided to throw a Christmas party for the refugees. After all, it was really their money: the purpose of the shop was not to turn a profit but to enable the refugees themselves to make a profit.

WE CALLED THE ENGABIRE BAKERY to place an order for a few large cakes for the party. As with a number of the projects comprising more than three people, disputes constantly broke out at the bakery, primarily over money and who was or was not working hard. Adding to their problems were difficulties in simply obtaining the necessary supplies. There was often no flour to be found in the city. Plastic bags used to wrap the loaves would suddenly disappear from store shelves. And if by chance there was sufficient flour and an adequate supply of bags, there might be no propane for the oven. For one three-month period, Agip, the local gas company, simply stopped selling propane. Engabire was forced to shut down; the women's income abruptly ceased.

After ironing out some of their interpersonal problems, the Engabire Bakery was finally making a go of it, selling bread to local Rwandese and even filling orders from religious communities: the Little Sisters of Jesus were happy to take three loaves each week; the Maryknoll Sisters, five; Hekima College, thirty; and the various JRS offices, ten. All of these orders were delivered by *matatu*. The bread (brown, white, or "mixed") was excellent, and home delivery more than made up for the extra shilling they charged over the going market price.

We had already started running monthly seminars for the refugees on how to run a business, and we covered accounting, marketing, and management. By far the most difficult concept to get across was pricing one's goods to include the cost of materials. The refugees would often charge less than it cost them to purchase materials, never understanding why they always seemed to lose money. During one session I explained to Kedress Kanzaire, the leader of the Engabire women, the necessity of counting every egg, every cup of flour, and every cup of sugar that went into each cake. That way, I explained, she wouldn't lose money on her baking.

After the course Kedress decided that her cakes would now cost 500 shillings, or about $10 US—an absurdly high amount, almost equivalent to two weeks rent. But rather than argue, I continued to buy the cakes: even if Kedress wasn't the most accurate cost accountant in the world, I reasoned the money was going to good use.

Towards the end of November, Kedress delivered a cake to our office, explaining that she noticed from her pocket calendar that it was American Thanksgiving. "And so," she said as she handed me the warm cake, "I am thanking *you* today, Brother!"

WE PLACED A SIGN in the main window announcing the Christmas party, and as with any of our notices, it was written in six languages: English, Swahili, French, Kinyarwanda, Luganda, and Amharic. The shop window had quickly become a kind of refugee bulletin board. Similarly, the porch had become a place to meet and trade news. As I pulled into the driveway each morning, I was always cheered to see refugees from so many ethnic groups—some of whom, like the Tutsi and Hutu, were often pitted against one another in their home countries—chatting away.

Occasionally only a few refugees visited the Mikono Centre (during the rains, for example), and I felt bad that those waiting on the porch had little to do. One day, in the office of St. Joseph the Worker Church, I noticed they sold all manner of inexpensive books. I bought a Swahili/English Bible and set it out on one of the benches. The next day I spied a Ugandan woman reading it intently. Eventually the benches were covered with Bibles in various languages, stories of the saints, Swahili and French magazines, coloring books and crayons for the children, and a few booklets on avoiding AIDS. Though a number of Jesuits cautioned me against setting out new books on our benches, the books remained intact. "Oh, Brother, *no one* would steal a Bible from you!" Alice Nabwire said when I remarked on the phenomenon.

Word of our Christmas party spread rapidly. Perhaps too rapidly: one refugee came in and reported, "All the refugees in the city are coming!" I knew that this was probably an exaggeration, but I began to worry nonetheless. I doubled the cake order.

A few days before the party, one of my Jesuit housemates, Angelo D'Agostino, called me. Angelo, a psychiatrist by training, had founded a center for children with AIDS in the city. His place, called *Nyumbani* ("at home") was located in Karen, a few hundred meters from the Jesuit retreat house there.

Angelo phoned to see if I might want some things that a donor had given him. What exactly was it? I asked.

He took a breath. "One thousand plastic cups, five hundred plastic plates, fifty jerrycans, and twenty buckets."

It wasn't a difficult decision; I said yes immediately. Any of the refugees, particularly the Ethiopian families who ran the restaurant projects, would be delighted with free plastic plates. Any of our five hair "saloons" would be happy to use the buckets for water. As for the jerrycans—the large plastic containers used for gasoline and water—they too would be snapped up quickly. None of the refugees I knew had running water in their houses. The one thousand cups would also be easy to get rid of. *Anything* was easy to give away in Kenya, since people had so little.

We decided to give the cups away as Christmas presents for our party.

Michael Schöpf and I drove over to Nyumbani in the jeep that afternoon. Angelo, all five feet six inches of him, ran out to greet us. He had a close-cropped white beard and a bald head. "Thank God you're here," he said. "These damn boxes are taking up too much room!" There were a number of small children tugging on his legs as he talked to us.

Angelo led us into a small windowless room where a seven-foot-high tower of colored plastic plates stood next to a large pile of green plastic buckets and black jerrycans. "And that," he said pointing to the corner, "is the box of cups." In the corner sat an immense box, about the size of a refrigerator. I let out a groan, wondering how we could fit everything into the jeep.

The plates and jerrycans we simply shoved, willy-nilly, into the back of the jeep. But we had to make another trip for the colossal box of cups. In the end, we ended up tearing open the box and simply dumping the one thousand green plastic cups into the jeep. As we bounced down Karen Road, hundreds of cups bounced into the air, flew up in front of us and onto the dashboard; some flew out of the car. From the rear view mirror I could see people running into the street to recover them. Merry Christmas.

A few days later, three Ethiopians visited us. They managed a restaurant called "The Blue Nile." (All of the Ethiopian restaurants in Nairobi seemed to be called either "Addis Ababa," after the capital, or "The Blue Nile." JRS sponsored two "Blue Niles.") The Blue Nile group happily took six buckets and asked for more. The other refugee groups eagerly accepted the rest of the largesse.

As the day of the party approached, the refugees began informing me what they were going to wear, and how many people they would bring to the *sharehe*, the party. I ordered six more cakes and began to consider whether we would need extra cases of soda. Yes, said a refugee nodding his head vigorously. "We will be *very* thirsty." In other matters, too, they offered suggestions.

"Will you be having music, Brother?" Gauddy Ruzage inquired a few days before the party. I hadn't really planned on it, I answered. She look shocked.

"On the other hand, I suppose I could find a tape recorder," I offered weakly. Gauddy smiled approvingly.

December 15, the day of the party, was clear and bright. Refugees began arriving at noon, even though we had listed two o'clock as the starting time. Most had little else to do, so why *not* come early? They spent the early afternoon on the porch reading books and magazines, playing with their children, weaving straw baskets and mats, telling stories, and laughing.

Soon I realized that, unlike a party in the States, where one serves food to guests who have probably already eaten that day, Michael and I were providing food to people who, in essence, never had enough to eat. So the dozen large cakes from the Engabire Bakery were wolfed down, and the thirty cases of soda seemed to evaporate. Scores of people camped out in the backyard, chatting and even singing in dozens of languages. I wanted to join them, but instead I spent most of the time snapping open Orange Fanta bottles and handing out pieces of warm cake on paper napkins.

But I was delighted that the refugees were having fun. Most of the refugees had few occasions to relax, and most were treated poorly in Nairobi, whether by their Kenyan neighbors, the police, or—more shockingly—by relief agencies where they were made to stand in line for hours. Their lives did not include people throwing parties for them.

An Ethiopian family approached me: Gebreselaissie, his wife, and his three children. Mrs. Gebreselaissie made beautiful shirts and dresses out of the fine white Ethiopian cotton, embroidered with multicolored yarn. She also made exquisite liturgical stoles—also in the Ethiopian style—with elaborate crosses that appealed particularly to French priests who visited the shop. Gebreselaissie himself produced stools fashioned from wooden dowels and tooled leather. He could make almost anything, he would say, and often asked if we were looking for new products for the shop. One day at the City Market in town, I happened upon one of the small, metal Ethiopian crosses often used as pendants or as ornaments for the house. I mentioned this to Gebreselaissie and asked if he knew how to make them. "Oh yes, Brother!" But the intricate crosses I had admired were made from poured tin or brass, and I wondered aloud if Gebreselaissie could find the right materials.

"Oh no, Brother, it is *very* easy!"

In a few days, however, he brought in a tin soda can fashioned into a cross. Not wanting to offend him, I purchased it but suggested that I liked his stools much more.

Gebreselaissie and his family now thanked me for the Christmas party, in the grave Ethiopian style: shaking my hand, while supporting their elbows with their left hands, while bowing at the waist. They thanked me in Amharic. The expression for "thank you" can be (loosely) transliterated as follows: "Ahmasegenalahu." It was one of my favorite East African words—it was so much fun to say—and I used it with Ethiopians at the drop of a hat. It rolled off the tongue like marbles.

"Before you leave," I said, "I have to give you your Christmas present." I went inside, lugged out the heavy cardboard box, and grabbed a trio of cups. Michael, Virginia, and I had spent the past few hours tying the cups in groups of three, one for each family—at least that's what we had planned. Inserted into each cup was a photocopied Christmas greeting in six languages.

Their eyes lit up as we handed them their green plastic cups. And so did the eyes of a few of the refugees behind them. Gebreselaissie and his family thanked me again, "Ahmasegenalahu!," bowed low, and exited.

Immediately a knot of refugees approached me. "Brother, what are those?" People began to stand up, staring. "What are those?" "What is it?" I made a sort of impromptu announcement.

"As a little Christmas gift we are happy to give you three plastic cups for each of your families!" I said.

Pandemonium. Dozens of refugees surged toward us with outstretched hands.

"But wait! Wait!" I shouted. "We'll give them out to you as you are leaving."

"We are leaving *now!*" they said as one.

And so Michael, Virginia, and I handed out dozens of cups to outstretched hands and watched helplessly as some of the refugees took the cups right out of the box.

"There are plenty for everyone!" I shouted over the din of voices, plastic cups clunking to the ground and cardboard tearing. "Just wait and you'll all get some!"

But it was no use. By now there were cups everywhere. I was beginning to grow frustrated.

"OK!" I finally yelled. "Will everyone please sit down?"

People stopped and stared at me.

"Sit down! *Please!*"

Slowly, everyone took their seats on the warm grass, a few holding their cups.

I addressed them in Swahili, grew even more flustered, and switched to English. "Look," I said. "We have one thousand cups. There are probably no more than two hundred people here, so there are *plenty* of cups to go around. So don't worry about getting them, OK?"

"Now," I continued. "I'll give out the rest of the cups to whatever families haven't received them. So who has already taken a cup?"

Not one hand was raised.

"Now, I know that we have given out about half the cups," I said evenly, "and that means that most of you here have gotten your cups. Raise your hands if you have."

"She has a cup, Brother!" one of the refugees pointed to another.

This was getting us nowhere.

"Please raise your hands if you've gotten a cup," I said. "There are *plenty* to go around."

A few hands were raised in the sea of people. My frustration grew. And then, quite spontaneously, I heard myself saying, "OK, I may not know who has those cups ... but *God* does!"

Suddenly, they burst into applause, apparently delighted at this theological insight. I wasn't sure if they were happy that I was finally being a hard-ass or impressed by my cleverness in confronting the situation. Probably a little of both. They whooped.

"That's right, Brother!" "Hooray for Brother Jim!" "Brother Jim is *right!*" "God will find the cups!" Then, as if on cue, a whole host of hands went up in the air.

I distributed the remainder of the cups. There were at least five hundred left over.

Everyone left happy, clutching their cups. "Merry Christmas, Brother!"

Michael and I laughed about the incident after everyone had left. Needless to say, we should have realized that here were people who had spent years in refugee camps where supplies of almost *anything* ran out. Better to be aggressive and get your family what they needed. I knew what the situation was like in the camps and had seen the lack of food and necessities, for example, at Thika. Their reaction was completely understandable; as on many occasions where the refugees had acted out of desperation or from their experience of poverty, Michael and I agreed that we would have done the same thing.

The next week we had some photos from the party developed. The refugees adored having their pictures taken, so I posted the photos in the main display room of Mikono Centre. One showed a Ugandan refugee named Samuel grinning, his arms affectionately thrown around his three small sons. In his hands he held what I counted to be fourteen cups. I had to admire his brazenness.

Samuel came in and regarded the picture. "Brother, can you be giving me a copy of this photo?"

"Samuel," I said solemnly. "What do you notice in this picture?"

"I am having a *good* time at your party, Brother," he said.

"And you also have fourteen cups, when the limit was three for one family."

"Ah," he said without missing a beat. "I was carrying the others for my friends."

NOT LONG AFTER the Christmas season, I visited a refugee in her house. In the middle of an otherwise bare table in her unlit wooden shack, occupying a place of some prominence, sat three of the green plastic cups. It was sad to think that something that would have been ignored at home, or perhaps thrown out— a plain plastic mug—was here so valued. But I was happy that we had been able to give them out. She saw me notice them.

"I am loving my Christmas cups," she said, and smiled.

OUR SPECIALITY

> Above all crops, teff (*Eragrostic teff*) drew the greatest attention of travelers and achieved pride of place across elite diets in the highlands. It was unique to Ethiopia, grew at elevations most traversed, appeared larger than life in Ethiopians' own conception of their cuisine, and was fed to honored guests as the primary ingredient of *enjera*, Ethiopia's distinctive, thin, fermented, batter "bread."
>
> —James McCann, *People of the Plow: Ethiopian Agriculture, 1890-1990.*

Restaurants were a popular project for Ethiopian refugees, and we sponsored three tiny restaurants in far-flung parts of Nairobi. Each one did a booming business, thanks to the thousands of Ethiopian refugees living in the city slums. JRS even sponsored an Ethiopian woman who made *enjera*—the Ethiopian staple—a pancake-like bread made from a bubbly, fermented batter of teff, a millet-like grain. Sara, working from her small shack in Dandora, did not lack for business.

One of the newest projects was "Addis Ababa," a restaurant

managed by three Ethiopian brothers and a sister, not far from the Jesuit community in Nairobi. The four constantly quarreled with their landlady and asked if I would speak with her. "We think she is a drug addict," they told me. I was surprised to discover that she was also an American, from North Carolina. She met me at the door of her flat in a pink chenille bathrobe and screamed that she was going to evict "those fucking Ethiopians." They were making too much noise, she said.

The Ethiopian brothers rolled their eyes when I passed on her comments. "*She* is the one who is noisy, Brother." I didn't doubt this; the Ethiopian refugees I knew were unfailingly polite and soft-spoken. It was difficult to imagine this group, or even their customers, making a ruckus.

After the landlady grudgingly agreed to extend their lease (and raise the rent after she met their white sponsor), Michael Schöpf and I were invited over for a meal. The Ethiopian restaurants in Nairobi served excellent fare, and you usually could get a tasty meal—as long as you avoided the mutton, which in Kenya was gamey, tough, and generally nasty.

The four brothers and their sister were lined up outside the restaurant when we arrived. They bowed low, embraced us, and escorted us inside, where the air was redolent with spicy *berbere* seasoning. They seated us at a low wooden table flanked by two tiny stools. We were given thin flasks of *t'ej*, a mead-like drink made of fermented honey. A menu was presented, handwritten in Amharic. There were seven entrees. I asked them to translate.

"We are somehow limited today in our food, Brother," said one brother apologetically. "This is mut-ton," he said deliberately, pointing to the first selection.

"And mut-ton," he said pointing to item #2.

"And mut-ton, mut-ton, mut-ton, mut-ton," he said, completing the menu.

Michael and I glanced at one another. One item remained. "And this?"

"Ah, our speciality, Brother." He smiled broadly. "Sheep intes-tines!"

Michael Coyne, courtesy of Black Star

Our destination was a refugee camp in the extreme north of Uganda, where tens of thousands of Sudanese refugees lived, and where the Jesuit Refugee Service team worked. Here, Father Celso Romanin, S.J., hears the confession of a Sudanese woman during a visit to one of the camps in the area.

ADJUMANI

For until you actually saw it and travelled across it on foot or on horseback or in a wagon, you could not possibly grasp the enormous vastness of Africa.

—Elspeth Huxley, *The Flame Trees of Thika*

The Christmas sale that year, which followed our little Yuletide party, proved very encouraging: we sold nearly half our stock. The Mikono Centre was finally becoming known throughout Nairobi. But it was also a tiring time, for when the refugees heard we had sold so many items, they knew that we would need to purchase more goods to replace the stock, and the number of refugees we saw in the following weeks skyrocketed. So Michael Schöpf suggested, one day after we had seen fifty refugees (we counted), that we should take a week's break and travel to northern Uganda. The JRS team there, who worked in a refugee camp near a town called Adjumani, had been pestering us—so far unsuccessfully—to visit them.

A short holiday would be a welcome break; we had had a

busy and successful Christmas season. It would also be a way to understand more of what some of the refugees endured during their long stays in the camps. Part of the allure of the trip, too, lay in its length. The twenty-six-hour train ride to Kampala, for example, sounded undeniably adventurous and was certainly the longest train trip I could imagine. Checking my plastic wall map of the continent, I discovered we would traverse a wonderfully diverse geography: the East African Railway snaked through the slums of Nairobi, crossed the Rift Valley, climbed past the cool tea plantations of the Highlands, crossed the Nile, and finally pulled into Kampala. Besides, the train was preferable to flying, which in East Africa was both dangerous and expensive.

The Nairobi-Kampala line had been out of service for nearly twenty years, a result of tensions between Kenya, Uganda, and Tanzania. This state of affairs was primarily the work of Idi Amin Dada, Uganda's former President for Life. By now, Amin had been in exile for some time, and Uganda, the "Pearl of Africa," as explorer Sir Henry Morton Stanley had called it, was led by a decidedly more progressive leader. Yoweri Museveni had brought his country closer to at least the possibility of good times. The *Daily Nation* had a few months earlier reported that Amin was now in exile in Saudi Arabia. They ran a picture of him, showing a still-imposing man in the clean white robe of a Muslim at prayer. "I am very devout now," he said in the article. But Amin or no, the byzantine politics of East Africa had kept the Nairobi-Kampala line in mothballs since the mid-1970s. Now, however, ads in the Kenyan papers trumpeted the reopening of the route, so it seemed an auspicious time for a trip to Uganda. Michael and I splurged for first-class tickets, which entitled us to share a small, two-person couchette.

Early on the morning of our trip we waited alongside of Ngong Road for a *matatu* headed for the center of town. The overcrowded bus finally pulled up, belching diesel fumes and broadcasting the sprightly guitar riffs of Zairian pop music. Each of the city's *matatus* had a name painted on the side, many reflecting a sort of half-knowledge of American or African-American culture. I seemed to get stuck behind "Michael Jordan" and "Bad Boyz" on the way to work every day. That morning, we caught "Two Live Crew." We squeezed on, ingratiating ourselves beside a man carrying a large chicken. In front of us was a Maasai man whose elongated earlobes looped over the top of his ears. The *tout*, or conductor, collected the fare of six shillings.

I had visited the old Kenyan Railways Station only once before. The station is the same as it was in colonial days—and as it was filmed for the movie *Out of Africa*—an elegant and elderly train shed supported by cream-colored pillars.

Michael and I chatted with some ticket-holders while we waited. Train rides are a rare treat for all but the wealthiest Kenyans, so the crowd was in high spirits. *Unaenda wapi?* Where are you going? one of them asked us. "Kampala," I answered. "Ah," he said approvingly, "*Safari mkubwa kabisa.*" A big trip indeed.

Presently, a curious person passed in front of our little group—a European or American man who had, as the settlers in Karen Blixen's time would say, "gone native." He was dressed as near as possible to a Maasai *moran*, or warrior. His otherwise straight Caucasian hair was plaited in tight cornrows. Around the young man's thin white shoulders hung the red *shuka* cloth of the Maasai. In a crook in his leather belt he carried a *rungu*, or fighting stick. He wore cheap rubber sandals made of old tires, like most of the Maasai men. I wondered what my Kenyan friends would say. After all, many Western missionaries aspired to become "inculturated," to insert themselves into the local culture by learning the language, understanding the customs, sharing the food. In this way a missionary could better understand the people with whom he worked. It was an admirable goal, one that sought to overcome the colonialist notion of the superiority of Western culture. And it was an approach I was comfortable with. But was it possible to become *too* inculturated?

I chanced some irony. "Look," I said in Swahili, "a Maasai."

"Ah," one of them said. "Ridiculous." The others roared with laughter. Inculturation to a point, I supposed. I remembered what a refugee had once asked me. "Brother, these Americans who are trying to be Africans. Do they forget who they are?"

The train appeared to have aged little in its twenty years in mothballs. Grimy and dusty in places, in spots clean paint shone, and the '70s-style accommodations looked surprisingly new. In our small compartment, two metal shelves pulled down to reveal vinyl-covered beds. A formica table-top concealed a tiny sink out of which water ran sporadically. Second class consisted of rows of comfortable seats, much like a commuter train in the States. Finally, third class, where the majority of the passengers traveled, consisted of rows of hard wooden slat benches.

As the train lurched out of Nairobi, the ancient steam whistle broke the hot bright air. A loud cheer arose from third class. "*Nenda, Nenda!*" Go, go!

People draped themselves out of the large windows. The train wound its way slowly through downtown Nairobi, affording us unusual views of the city: the grimy backs of office buildings, their windows open, with dirty curtains billowing out like old handkerchiefs; the debris along the railroad tracks; looming clouds heralding a late-afternoon shower.

Within minutes we drew into the slums that ring Nairobi, a city that itself is three-quarters slum. Countless wooden shacks held together with mud stretched before us, surrounding Nairobi Dam—the source of the water supply that occasionally found its way to the wealthier parts of the city. Thin trails of white smoke rose from where people roasted corn. Laundry hung limply from strings and wires stretched between the houses. Everywhere people meandered aimlessly. Passengers in third class called out to the people in the slums, and, in a sight we would see repeated throughout the trip, people ran from their shacks up to our train shouting greetings: "*Jambo treni!*" Hello train!

After settling in to our compartment, we explored the train. The corridors were packed with people—*matatu* style—leaning out of the windows, a hazardous venture as soot poured forth from the smokestacks, covering everything with the fine black powder. We were, we noticed, the only whites on the train.

A conductor arrived to collect our tickets and explain the procedures for meals. Breakfast, lunch, and dinner were to be served in the dining car. A man would strike a set of chimes to announce the seating for dinner. A Ugandan couple stopped by our compartment. Had we ever been to Uganda? they asked. They were on the last leg of a long safari that had taken them into Tanzania. Would we join them for dinner? A Kenyan man stopped by, evidently surprised to see a *mzungu,* a white person. *Unaenda wapi?* Where are you going? Most of our fellow travelers were visiting relatives in Uganda.

An immense plain suddenly stretched before us—the Rift Valley, the wide swath of land that slices through East Africa, north to south. It is the vista of terrain that many people think of when they imagine East Africa: an endless, flat, parched plain, with hundreds of gazelles sleeping in the distance. This was, of course, the same vista that attracted intrepid riders to the railway in the early part of the twentieth century. Charles Miller's book, *The Lunatic Express,* nicely captures the allure:

> *Braving the showers of red-hot embers that poured from the locomotive smokestack, passengers climbed onto the roofs of their carriages for an unobstructed view of the most massive and varied assemblage of game species anywhere on earth. . . . The zebra nearest the tracks might raise their heads momentarily as the train thundered by, but would return at once to munching the grass, altogether unperturbed.*

The porter dropped by our compartment to ask us if we wanted any food. His dress was a combination of English propriety (a short white coat and white pants) and African reality (both his coat and pants were torn and his worn rubber sandals showed his dusty feet).

At lunchtime, Michael and I settled into the dining car,

which swayed back and forth as we climbed higher and higher into the tea country north of Nairobi. The train slowed as it struggled up the winding hillsides.

Across from us sat a prosperous-looking Kenyan gentleman. On the stiff white tablecloth sat heavy silver cutlery, flanked by chipped china plates, all bearing the logo "East African Railway," and all dating from colonial days. After some pleasantries we discussed the menu. Chicken marengo, *ugali* and *sukuma*, and chicken curry were the choices.

"How's the food on this train?" I asked tentatively. "Do you think it's all right to eat?" I figured that if it was difficult to get decent food in Nairobi proper, then on a train, well . . .

"Actually, quite good," he said.

Michael looked doubtful.

"I should know," the man laughed. "I'm the Inspector of Health for Kenya Railways."

True to the health inspector's promise, the fare was excellent. "Next time you can be ordering the curry," he said as he tucked into his own meal. "My wife gave them the recipe."

The Nairobi-Kampala train ran only once a week, so our visit was something of an event in the small villages we passed through. "*Mzungu! Mzungu! Mzungu!*" cried the barefoot children who came tearing out of their dirt huts as the train passed, using the East African word for any white person.

There were a number of explanations for the word's provenance. The most satisfying was that *mzungu* is the Swahili term for a traffic roundabout. The natives found this British innovation so unusual that they began to use it to describe them. ("Roundabout," a Kikuyu woman told me early on, is also a good way to describe the way Westerners think.) Similarly, the word was used as the root of an all-purpose term to describe the language of any Westerner: *kizungu*. I had, on occasion, heard rural Kenyans saying "*Sifahamu kizungu,*" in other words, "I don't speak Western." That particular term, I thought, was a just payback for Westerners who would ask me if it was difficult to learn how to speak "African."

As the train climbed into the Kenyan Highlands, it became progressively cooler; the air was fresher and cleaner than I had expected. In his book *Remote People*, which detailed his visit to British East Africa in the 1930s, Evelyn Waugh noted this about the climate in the Highlands: "Brilliant sunshine quite unobscured, uninterrupted in its incidence; sunlight clearer than daylight; there is something of the moon about it, the coolness seems so unsuitable."

A dazzling, emerald carpet stretched before us in undulating waves. Hundreds of tea pickers bent over the endless fields of the tea plantations. Finally, we pulled even higher into banks of evergreen trees. "This looks like Bavaria," Michael commented. Maine, I thought. Or the Adirondacks.

When we returned to our compartment after dinner we discovered that clean white sheets had been placed on the vinyl seats. We settled in for the night. By now it was completely dark outside, and stars filled an utterly black sky.

In the middle of the night we passed into Uganda and were jolted awake by the porter. "Tororo! Tororo!" he shouted. Until this point, my experience with crossing the border by train, at least in Europe, consisted of handing over one's passport to a porter who would take care of business as one slept. In East Africa, however, one is expected to rouse oneself, leave the train, and stand in a long line in the cold darkness. A sullen and sleepy Ugandan official stamped a pale purple triangle in our passports that said, "Tororo, Uganda." The train started up, and we were returned to sleep by its gentle rocking.

In the morning we drew the shades; blinding sunshine filled our room. We were faced with tall green plants moving in the hot breeze, as far as the eye could see in any direction—papyrus flowers, swaying on slim, reedy stalks in the marshes. As the train, chased by Ugandan children, made its way through the country, the ravages of Amin's time presented themselves. Telephone poles—tree trunks really—stood helplessly along the tracks with wires hanging limply down their sides. Decrepit concrete buildings were riddled with bullet holes. The Pearl of Africa. In a few hours, we passed the waterfalls at Jinja, the traditional "Source of the Nile" that the British explorers Sir Richard Francis Burton and John Hanning Speke had sought in the 1850s.

Tall thin plants swayed on surprisingly delicate stems in the wind. "This is cassava," the staple of diets in Uganda and western Kenya, said the porter as he passed by me carrying Fantas, another dietary staple.

KAMPALA WAS MUCH DUSTIER than Nairobi and less cosmopolitan. Like the rest of the country it had suffered grievously under Idi Amin and the brutal civil war that had followed his overthrow. The modest sandstone train station was pockmarked with bullet holes, its walls chipped on all sides from machine-gun fire.

The three Jesuits who met us at the station drove us through the dusty streets to Xavier House, a community of about fifteen Jesuits who worked in various ministries in Kampala. One Jesuit physician worked at Makerere University running an AIDS clinic and doing research on the disease (which is known as "slim" in Uganda). A few hundred meters away, two Jesuit novices worked in Nsambya Hospital, a hospital almost entirely devoted to caring for AIDS patients. Even if I hadn't heard stories of how AIDS had decimated Uganda's population, it would have been driven home by the sight of coffin-makers on nearly every street corner in Kampala. Plain wooden caskets were stacked up, sometimes ten high, along every roadside. In many towns in Uganda, there was a surfeit of what they called "AIDS orphans," children who had lost both parents to the illness.

Xavier House was similar to many religious houses scattered throughout East Africa. Its rooms were organized, monastery style, around an ample courtyard of palm trees, spindly rose bushes, orange bird-of-paradise plants, spiky green sisal and aloe plants, and bougainvillea. A living room, dining room, and a large circular chapel (whose altar was an enormous Ugandan drum) completed the community. Their small garden boasted, among other things, fourteen different types of banana trees, the fruits of which were available in straw baskets in the dining room. Also on the dining room tables were ceramic bowls generously filled with small white pills—chloroquine, an antimalarial medication—for daily use by community members.

Midway through a week of touring Kampala, Michael and I decided to purchase our return tickets at the Kampala train station. A sign reading "Tickets" marked a room completely empty but for a large trestle table. On top of the table lay a woman, supine, in a flowered cotton dress, sleeping in the middle of the morning.

"Excuse me," I said.

She roused herself. "Huh?"

"We'd like to buy tickets for next week's return trip," Michael said hopefully.

"This is quite impossible," she said as she sat up. She rubbed her eyes and smoothed out her dress. "We don't sell them until next Tuesday."

"The day before the train?"

"Yes, we must be sure that this train has left Nairobi, before we can be selling tickets."

We considered this. "What about a reservation?"

A napkin that had been blowing across the dusty floor settled by her foot. She picked it up. "What is your name?"

I told her. She wrote it on the napkin.

"What date do you want to be leaving?"

"Hmm . . . let's see." Across the room I spied a wall calendar with Idi Amin's portrait. I couldn't quite figure out the dates. Today was Tuesday, right? And wasn't it the fifteenth? So, why was the fifteenth a Wednesday? Eventually, I noticed that the calendar was from 1975. This probably wouldn't help. So I just said next Tuesday.

She wrote this down and placed the dirty napkin in a drawer in the table. "Now," she said confidently, "You are reserved." Then she climbed onto the table and rolled over.

The next day we prepared for our flight to Adjumani, in the extreme north of Uganda. We would be flying via "Mission

Aviation Fellowship," a Lutheran-based organization that shuttled pastoral care workers, Red Cross employees, and dozens of UN personnel around the country. Everyone knew it as MAF. Flying in these tiny MAF planes was the only way to get around the country. So in the cool Ugandan dawn we met a small bus which took us to the house of the pilot, an RAF veteran. From there we drove to Entebbe Airport.

I found the prospect of traveling from Entebbe enormously interesting. I remembered the aborted PLO hijacking in the mid-1970s and the spectacular Israeli raid on the airport. And just in case I had forgotten, Kenyan television aired the schlocky TV-movie *Raid on Entebbe* almost monthly. I briefly wondered whether there would be any sign of the plane, but I brushed the thought away. After all, it was more than twenty years ago.

We neared the airport which, strangely, was ringed by a high stockade fence, painted a dull green, that prevented one from seeing anything. Through a break in the fence I spied a rusting plane sitting forlornly on the runway. "Oh," mentioned the pilot in passing, "that's that plane from the Israelis."

So there it was. The plane sat beside the old airport terminal, looking just like it did in the movie, wounded by explosives; through the collapsed roof of the terminal, tall palm trees grew. "They couldn't move the plane after the hijacking of course, and it would have been too costly to tear down the terminal, so they just built that one over there." He pointed to a newer, smaller building.

"Which hijacking was that?" Michael asked.

"Oh, please," I replied, shocked. "Raid on Entebbe!" Apparently German TV didn't air the movie as often as American or Kenyan TV.

There were, of course, no bags checked at Entebbe. We simply walked from our car to the plane. The only formality was weighing ourselves on a small plastic bathroom scale, in order to determine whether we would be too heavy for the plane. For someone who loathes flying as much as I do, this homey procedure did not inspire much confidence. Nor did the sight of the plane: a tiny five-seater, dwarfed on the runway by an Ethiopian Air jet parked beside it. "You're pretty light," said our pilot. "You can sit in back."

I climbed into the tiny plane, which seemed, if possible, even smaller and flimsier on the inside. Through the detritus inside—blankets, maps, cans of food, bottles of water, an emergency first-aid kit—the pilot struggled to hand me a styrofoam picnic cooler.

"What's this?" I asked.

"Blood," he said. "We're bringing some to the Red Cross in Zaire."

We were going to Zaire?

In a few minutes Michael, myself, a Red Cross worker, a UNICEF doctor, and a representative from the Ugandan government were all crammed into the MAF plane. This being "Mission Aviation Fellowship," the pilot led us in a brief prayer. "Please keep us safe through this journey, God, and get us to our destination so we can do your work. Please don't let the fuel cap fall off like it did the last time. Amen." I hoped that God would watch over us, particularly the fuel cap. The plane engine started. It was deafening, and the plane jiggled and bounced down the runway, reminding me briefly of my jeep. Suddenly we lurched up, passing over an Ethiopian Air jet, the new terminal, and the damaged Israeli jet. Looking straight down, we could peer through the destroyed roof of the old terminal.

In a few minutes, we were flying over the lush Ugandan jungle. "That's the Luwero Triangle!" the pilot shouted. He pointed. Ugandan refugees in Nairobi spoke of this place often. The triangle, once home to nearly one million members of the Baganda tribe, had in the early 1980s found itself at the center of a civil war. In a five-year period beginning in 1981, the Ugandan military sealed off the Luwero Triangle, razed villages, murdered an estimated quarter million people, and sent the rest into the bush or to concentration camps. Now, all one could see was the intense green of the jungle and the tiny grey shadow of our plane.

Though the view was spectacular as we passed over Lake Albert ("Lake Mobutu Sese Seko" on the Zairian side), I looked forward intensely to landing. The plane now rattled and chugged ominously.

Our first stop was just across the Zairian (now Congolese) border, where we would drop off the supply of blood. "There's the landing field," yelled the pilot over the din.

Where? I looked down, and I saw nothing. The earth drew closer and closer, and we landed with a metallic thud. The landing field was precisely that: a field where we landed. Bags, boxes, and maps flew into the air. The picnic cooler of blood flew out of my hands and narrowly missed bumping into the ceiling. Out of the bush a man dashed toward the plane. "Give me the blood!" said the pilot. Without turning off the engines the MAF pilot handed him the picnic cooler, and we were off again.

Soon we were chugging our way over more jungle, more *shambas*, and more undulating hills. We ran into towering clouds. "We're going around!" our pilot yelled, and the plane tipped dramatically. Empty soda bottles flew against the inside of the plane.

After another hour of clear flying, we reached Adjumani. As there was no radio in town, we circled over the small town to let our friends know we had arrived. Far below us I saw people emerge from their houses, wave up in the air, and climb into their Land Rovers. Our small plane clumped down onto a rocky field. Terrifically hot dry air blew through dried brown grass. "Not bad," said the pilot to no one in particular.

"Why did we go around those clouds?" I asked, tentatively.

"No radar. There's no telling what's in those clouds," he answered laughing. "Birds, planes, whatever. . . . " He trailed off absentmindedly and began to inspect the plane.

Our friends arrived via Land Rover in a few minutes. Sister Maureen, the intrepid Australian sister, bounded out of the car. "Well, good on ya! You made it, then," she shouted. "It's rather a dull trip, isn't it?"

In a few minutes we reached Adjumani, a tiny village that

looked like most of the small Kenyan towns I had seen. Poured concrete structures, boarded-up stores with tin roofs, people wearing torn clothes meandering through the dirt streets.

The JRS compound was near the center of town, surrounded by a low fence. In the middle of the compound stood a small concrete bungalow surrounded by Sudanese style *tukels*—dirt huts with thatched roofs. The team had erected another small house as a sort of office, outfitting it with an electric generator to power up an old computer and a short-wave radio that kept them in touch with the main community in Kampala.

The community was an unusual mix of Jesuit priests and scholastics (Australian, American, Ethiopian), sisters (two Australians and one American), an American diocesan priest, and one layperson (German), all living together, eating together, and working with the thousands of Sudanese refugees in the camps a few kilometers away. It was an innovative way of living for a religious community. (Some Jesuit communities in Europe, for example, still place minor restrictions on where women can and cannot go.) It made me proud to see the East African Jesuits taking the lead.

The JRS team lived and worked in a situation of considerable physical danger. The Sudanese People's Liberation Army, the military organization of the South, had splintered into at least three factions; fighting among them broke out regularly. Worse, groups of Ugandan rebels and bandits, some loyal to President Yoweri Museveni in Kampala, others to local faction leaders, others professing no allegiance to anyone but themselves, regularly robbed, beat, and killed local Ugandans, Sudanese refugees, and aid workers. The week before I had arrived, three of the JRS team had been ambushed. Sister Margaret, an Australian Sister of Mercy, told me the story my first night in their dining tent, by the light of a hissing kerosene lamp.

She had been bringing food supplies to one of the refugee camps with Celso, the Australian Jesuit who served as director of the work in Adjumani, and Kessy, a young Tanzanian Jesuit. In the Land Rover they carried a number of large sacks of maize meal and flour. The three bounced over the bumpy Ugandan roads. Suddenly a young man with a rifle leaped out in front of their jeep, motioning for them to stop. They knew, however, that stopping and handing over the jeep did not guarantee their safety.

Initially, Sister Margaret slowed down, but as they drew nearer to the man, she gunned the engine.

As the car accelerated the bandit opened fire. "He was quite young," explained Sister Margaret, "and probably couldn't hold the machine gun very well." Machine gun fire sprayed the car. In the midst of the gunfire, the Land Rover hit a large bump, throwing the passengers into the air. They sped away, terrified; but only Celso had been hit, in his forearm.

Later that day in the compound, after tending to Celso's wounds, they inspected the Land Rover for damage. They discovered that, somehow, the bullets had lodged in the truck's seats or in the sacks of flour stored behind the seats. At first, they couldn't understand how the bullet holes could have ended up in places where they had been seated. To do so the bullets would have had to pass through their bodies. Eventually, they realized that the bullets penetrated the Land Rover at precisely the moment they hit the big bump. In other words, as the three were lifted from their seats—by the force of the truck hitting the bump—the bullets passed under them, through the seats, and into the sacks of flour. Margaret, Celso, and Kessy were all convinced it was something of a miracle. Or maybe precisely a miracle.

WHILE THE MAIN HOUSE in Adjumani was considerably more comfortable than the outlying *tukels*, it had no running water or electricity. The lack of electricity didn't seem to present much of a problem for the team. Meals were cooked over a charcoal fire, and the day ended at sunset. Obtaining water, on the other hand, was more of an ordeal. Every day they drove to the village spring to fetch water with buckets and jerrycans. The drinking water had to be filtered and boiled; what remained was used for showers and the washing of clothes. The house had a toilet, a remnant of the pre-Amin days when there was running water in Adjumani. Now the toilet was flushed with a bucket of spring water. But most of the time you used the outhouse which consisted of a hole in the ground surrounded by a wooden shack. The water situation, I reflected, might take some getting used to.

A few months earlier, Mary Pat Loftus and I had traveled to Nakuru, some fifty kilometers north of Nairobi, to visit some volunteer friends who worked for the Christian Brothers in a technical school. They, too, had to boil their water and filter it with an elaborate contraption that made one think twice before wasting anything. This was one benefit of living in Nairobi: the water was (more or less) clean. On the other hand, during my first October there had appeared in the *Daily Nation* a notice informing readers that for the last three months, the water in the city had not been treated. In other words, we had been drinking with no ill effects water straight from Lake Nairobi, where people also defecated and washed their clothes.

An American Jesuit with whom I lived had, as a sort of experiment, set a glass of Nairobi tap water on his windowsill and watched all sorts of—in his words—"critters" grow in the glass. And true, most visitors to Nairobi fell ill from what we suspected was the water. But we were grateful that long-time residents seemed to develop a tolerance. Once outside of Nairobi, however, indeed in almost any other place in East Africa boiling and filtering were a necessity.

The difficulty of living in a place like Adjumani was readily apparent. In addition to the challenges of water and electricity there was also the stifling heat and, especially, the dust. In Nairobi, the red dirt of the city covered your pants and shoes twenty-four hours a day; in the rainy season you scraped off only with great difficulty the sticky mud from the bottom of your sneakers or gumboots. Here in Adjumani it was dust: a fine brown silt that swirled about in the fetid air, getting into your eyes, your nose, your mouth. I was cleaning it out of my clothes for weeks afterwards.

The first night I slept in one of the *tukels*. "Slept" is probably not the correct phrase. More accurate is to say that I "passed the night" under my torn mosquito netting listening to huge bugs buzz around the *tukel*, crash noisily into the net, and bite me when they could. As I had discovered earlier in Mombasa, the mosquito nets kept only the larger bugs away and made the hot night even stuffier.

The next day Michael and I visited the camps, where hundreds of thousands of southern Sudanese lived in dusty blue UN tents huddled under a scorching sun. My first vista of the camp was quite literally breathtaking: an entire city of refugees stretched out before us on the dry plain as far as I could see, the vista broken only by clouds of yellow dust and thin white trails of smoke that coiled up from the cooking fires. Sister Margaret showed us around one of the camps, and we walked through slowly, greeting people along the way. Up close, the camp looked like the slums in Nairobi, except that here in Adjumani there was little apparent activity. The refugees seemed simply to be waiting, and a cloudy torpor seemed to hang over the camp.

The week moved on slowly and deliberately, like the rest of life in Adjumani. One morning, we made a visit to one of the schools run by JRS, where hundreds of Sudanese children sat silently on plain benches under a tree. Another day, we visited the Nile at dusk, where women drew water with clay jugs, while unseen baboons screamed in the fading light. On Sunday, our last day, Celso celebrated Mass for a handful of refugees under a large tree. A slight breeze blew, rustling dead leaves and raising clouds of dust. Their simple intercessory prayers went on for thirty minutes. I pray for my father who is dead, said one refugee. I pray for my mother who is very sick. I pray to find my children, who are lost.

On Monday we left, flying back in the tiny MAF plane to Entebbe, and, finally, boarding the Nairobi train in Kampala, where, I was surprised to discover, they had reserved our tickets after all.

HURRY, HURRY, MEANS NO BLESSINGS

> Proverbs are a mirror in which a community can look at itself and a stage on which it exposes itself to others.
>
> —Patrick A. Kililombe, quoted in
> *Towards an African Narrative Theology*

The everyday greeting in Kenya is *"Jambo,"* which while implying a general "Hello" has another connotation. It is the Swahili word for "problem." And so the salutation *"Jambo?"* can also be taken as, "Do you have any problems?" The normal response was just *"Jambo"* in return, but sometimes *"Nyingi."* Many. I have many problems.

A problem was also known as *shida* or *matata*. Fans of the Disney movie *The Lion King* will be happy to know that *hakuna matata* really does mean "no worries," but that the less musical expression *hakuna shida* is more common. The fact that there are so many words for problems or worries goes a long way to describing life in Kenya, like the old saw that the Eskimo has a hundred words for snow. East Africa, the cradle of humanity, sometimes seemed to be the cradle of problems and snafus.

Of course, there are the larger problems, *mashida makubwa*: poverty, sickness, homelessness, hunger, violence, political instability. These were the problems that the refugees faced daily. (Add to this rather incomplete list harassment from the police and the local Kenyans.) But the *shidas* that were the more frequent objects of conversation were the smaller ones prevalent in any poor nation crippled by corruption and colonialism: cars that don't start, lights that don't light, windows that don't close, buses that don't run, offices that don't open (with workers who don't work). And so on.

As a result the most commonly used Swahili expression in Kenya, by far, was *pole* (pronounced "poh-lay"), a sort of all-purpose "sorry." It is unique in its ability to be used for nearly every occasion, from stubbing one's toe ("*Pole*, Brother!"), to breaking a glass, to graver affairs like the loss of a job, serious illness, even the death of a spouse. Interestingly, the term *pole pole* was used to mean "slow" or, sometimes, "slow down." Whenever I asked the refugees how their businesses were faring, the inevitable response was *Tunaendelea pole pole*: "We are pushing on slowly, slowly." A sign on Waiyaki Way alerting motorists to oncoming road construction read, "*Pole Pole*." Slow down. After a few months of road construction, the sign was broken in two, one half remained. It read simply, "*Pole*." Sorry.

In fact, the preponderance of screw-ups and snafus gave rise to an expression among some expat workers: "Africa Wins Again." This was used when you assumed you'd be able to complete a task as you had planned, on time or in the way you wanted. You plan to rise early in order to arrive at work early. But the water tank in your house did not fill overnight, and so you have no running water. It takes you thirty minutes to take a cold shower out of a bucket; you end up being even later than usual. "Africa Wins Again," your friend will say when you finally do arrive.

"Oh no," was the refrain of Virginia, a kind young Kenyan woman who cleaned our office. Her tremendously understated "Oh no's," coming in response to unforeseen difficulties, punctuated my time in Kenya. One morning as Virginia and I opened the Mikono Centre, we noticed water trickling from under the door. Together we stepped into the shop, onto parquet floors covered with an inch of dirty water. "Oh no," said Virginia. The previous day, Virginia had turned on the faucets, but our tanks were empty. No water. Unfortunately, she had neglected to turn them off again, and when the tanks filled overnight, so did the sink, and then, the floor. It ruined anything that we were displaying on the floor—straw mats, baskets, rugs.

Shortly after we moved into the Mikono Centre, I asked a local *fundi*, or workman, to affix a metal gate onto the back door. Robberies were common in Kangemi, and we had not only the refugee goods to worry about, but also a personal computer and a cash box, both within plain view of anyone who visited the shop. One afternoon after returning from visiting a refugee, I came upon the *fundi* on the back porch, packing up his tools. Virginia was cleaning up some of the stone chips that had fallen on the ground, since the *fundi* had bored deep holes into the outer wall of the house. "*Kwisha!*" he said triumphantly. Finished!

Something seemed awry though. As he described how strong the bars were, I tried opening the gate. It opened in, toward the house. Unfortunately, the door of the house opened *out*. Which meant that the door was now unusable. "Oh no," said Virginia, as she watched me open the gate and bang it into the open house door.

"Now, what do you think about this, *Bwana?*" I asked the *fundi*. "No one can get out now."

"Yes, Brother," he said happily. "And no one can be getting in, either!"

Paradoxically, all of these little *shidas* gave rise to a more human, more accepting way of looking at life. Everyone expects things to go wrong, to be late, and so when they do, there is no big fuss. My jeep used to regularly break down, overheat, and suffer tire punctures, necessitating numerous unforeseen visits to Mr. A.P. Singh's BP station, which in turn caused me to be late for appointments at Mikono. But the refugees were never cross. *Hakuna shida,* Brother!

Likewise, I learned not to be upset myself if I was kept waiting for an hour or two—or even a day or two. I knew there would be a good excuse, and they would eventually come. *Pole pole,* the refugees would tell me. Slowly, slowly.

Ultimately, I began to realize that the refugees were probably right. Why spend your time worrying about someone being late? Things will eventually get done. What's the hurry? Or as Virginia used to remind me, *Haraka haraka, haina baraka,* which can be loosely translated as, "Hurry, hurry, means no blessings."

SOME LITTLE MONEY

> The fruitfulness of our life depends in large measure on our ability to doubt our own words and to question the value of our own work. The man who completely trusts his own estimate of himself is doomed to sterility.
>
> —Thomas Merton, *New Seeds of Contemplation*

By January of my second year, I had reached the point where I felt at home in Kenya. Life at the Mikono Centre was something I enjoyed; I had come to know hundreds of refugees, their children, their spouses, their neighborhoods, and their concerns. It seemed as much of a home to me as my Jesuit community. I was also fortunate to come to know an Irish family living in the nearby town of Karen, who frequently opened their home to Jim Corrigan, Michael Schöpf, and me. Spending time with Mike and Jacinta Dixon at their gracious house was a much-needed tonic for working in the slums. Jacinta also helped Mikono Centre by occasionally manning our booth at the Nairobi bazaars that were becoming a more frequent event for us.

Another new friend was Domatila Kieti, the receptionist at the Jesuit community. Domatila, it turned out, was the perfect guide through Kenyan society. If a particular cultural nicety or East African tradition puzzled me, Nairobi-born Domatila was always eager to furnish an answer. How to shake hands properly, the correct way to consume various Kenyan foods, the distinctions among the various ethnic groups in her country, as well as any linguistic challenges (she taught me a few handy Kikuyu greetings that never failed to impress); all fell under Domatila's considerable purview. It had also fallen to her at the beginning of my stay to assist me in my bout with *Hodi?* and *Karibu*.

Domatila was also the first Kenyan to invite me to her home for a meal. She evidently spent the entire day preparing for the visit; dinner consisted of *ugali, sukuma,* beef stew, salad (which in Kenya meant a small mountain of shaved carrots topped with a dollop of mayonnaise), and *chapatis,* the flat flour pastries cooked in an open skillet. During the meal she mentioned that *chapatis* were a delicacy traditionally served on Christmas Day in Kenya. When I remarked on how unusual it was that an Indian dish would be a Kenyan specialty, Domatila evinced horror. *Chapatis,* she insisted, were *Kenyan.* Her guest decided it was more gallant to let her win the argument.

I had also found what is known in religious circles as a "spiritual director," someone with whom I could discuss my spiritual life, most especially prayer. In my case it was a Jesuit priest named George Drury, an American who worked at the Jesuit retreat house in Karen. The retreat house, called *Mwangaza* (after the Swahili word for "light") was situated on a portion of what was formerly the estate of Karen Blixen, the author of *Out of Africa.* In fact, the retreat house itself was originally built by the subsequent owners of Baroness Blixen's estate. They had found her modest house too small.

Mwangaza is set on a considerable parcel of land at the foot of the Ngong Hills, and I considered the view from the back yard to be the loveliest vista in all of East Africa. In the foreground was a superb garden of bird-of-paradise plants, pink geraniums, gardenias, hibiscus bushes, bottlebrush trees, palm trees, and tall Norfolk pines. In the distance towering eucalyptus trees, their delicate scent perfuming the air, framed the pale blue Ngong Hills. Brilliant turacos and sunbirds chattered; an occasional hummingbird splashed in the stone birdbath in the center of a sunny courtyard. I went to Mwangaza every two weeks for direction, and George Drury, an avuncular New Englander, exerted an influence on my spiritual life as calming as the mountain breezes that blew through the garden.

I was exceedingly grateful for the support of all these people—Mike and Jacinta Dixon, Domatila Kieti, George Drury, and my Jesuit and expat friends—since at the time I faced one of the most difficult episodes during my stay in Kenya. It centered on a man named Benjamin Mugabo.

IN A COUNTRY of sad people, Benjamin, a young Rwandese man, was one of the saddest refugees I knew. Since he was nearly always sick it was difficult to determine his age; perhaps he was twenty, perhaps thirty. He was painfully thin, skeletal really, and his enormous brown eyes were always rheumy and bloodshot. Each time we met, Benjamin would be wearing the same clothes—what I came to realize were his *only* clothes—a torn white shirt, dirty blue polyester pants, and thin-soled sandals wrapped with cracked, yellowing adhesive tape.

Benjamin had started visiting when I was still working out of Sister Luise's office. "Brother, I am sick a bit today," he would say in a scratchy voice and request money for the local health clinic. He suffered, he said, from painful stomach ulcers, and the medication was very expensive. A doctor's prescription would be produced. And could he also have some money for food? "Some little money," he would say.

He said he had no family. They, Tutsis, had all been killed in Rwanda years ago. Whether or not this was accurate was, like his age, difficult to ascertain. Benjamin was unmarried and lived alone in a tiny wooden shack across town, in Ngando, near Alice Nabwire. I noticed that when he visited Mikono Centre some of the other Rwandese avoided him. He was, as far as I could tell, seen as a slight embarrassment to the more hard-working members of their group.

When he heard that we were sponsoring people for businesses, he immediately made application for one. But sadly, Benjamin seemed to have no skills or experience in any sort of trade, craft, or business. Despite this, he regularly submitted proposals for opening a hotel, a restaurant, a carpentry shop, a mechanic's workshop, a printing press, all written in his own shaky hand on dirty, creased paper. Each time we were forced to turn him down—as Benjamin had no discernible experience in any of these businesses. Each time he hung his head and asked the same question: "But what can I do?"

When we moved to Kangemi to open the Mikono Centre, Benjamin showed up a few days later asking for some little money. He had heard that we were now selling refugee-made crafts. And so Benjamin brought hand-made products of his own, items that he had quite obviously never made before. Some of the refugees, for example, made exquisite banana-leaf note cards, delicate dried brown leaves carefully fashioned into pictures of African women, the Holy Family, and assorted wild animals. One day Benjamin brought three cards with chopped-up banana leaves clumsily stuck onto the paper with large clumps of white paste. I gave him a few shillings for his cards, but when he asked if I wanted to order more I had to say no.

Soon Benjamin began showing up at Mikono every day, asking for money. Usually I gave him some from my own pocket. It was clear he had nowhere else to go.

In time I realized that it would be easier simply to hire Benjamin—and probably cheaper—but as what? We already employed Virginia, a hard-working and personable young woman from Kangemi, to help clean the shop and Marie Bugwiza, a well-educated Rwandese refugee, as a saleswoman. Before she departed for Germany, Uta had also hired an Ethiopian man named Berehe as a groundskeeper. But Berehe was quite elderly and able to do precious little work. He seemed to spend much of the day, in fact, smoking on the porch and chatting with the other refugees. Perhaps Benjamin could help out as a sort of assistant groundskeeper, to water the plants, tend the large garden around the house, and carry out the heavy work that Berehe was often unable to do. Benjamin wept when I proposed this job. "Yes, yes," he said, "I can be doing that, Brother."

But Benjamin's difficulties continued unabated. On his first day of work I asked him to weed our small garden. Perhaps, I suggested, he should wear "gumboots," the high rubber boots that Kenyans wore during the rainy season and when working in their *shambas*. Benjamin stared at the floor. "Yes, Brother, but I don't have these gumboots." He had only his one pair of torn sandals. So we bought him gumboots. We purchased him a hat as well, to protect him from the *jua kali*, the hot sun.

Coincidentally, around the same time we hired Benjamin, another refugee began visiting us, an older Sudanese fellow named Elijah who made a living selling plants and trees. Every week Elijah would pedal in on a decrepit bicycle and offer us a dogeared list of the types of plants he could provide. Bird of Paradise: Ksh. 250. Geranium: Ksh. 50. Irises: Ksh. 100. Bougainvillea: Ksh. 100.

As with Benjamin, I felt sorry enough for him that, even though we had no need for more plants, I purchased something from Elijah every week. In a few days he would return on his bike, toting a small plant or tree wrapped in an old newspaper. "Ha!" said Alice Nabwire when she first spied him bringing in one of the plants. "He is probably stealing them from someone's garden." In any event, Elijah's plants gave Benjamin something to do. And in a few months, thanks to Benjamin, Elijah, and the rains, the garden that surrounded Mikono Centre exploded with a variety of flowering plants. One British woman, a gardener by avocation, pronounced our irises the best she had seen *anywhere*.

Along with Marie, Virginia, and Berehe, Benjamin took his lunch at Mikono Centre. It was cheap to provide meals for the four, just a few shillings a day, and Virginia was a clever and resourceful cook. The four, though from different backgrounds, were beginning to form a tight-knit group.

But besides a desultory schedule of planting, Benjamin did little work. When asked to clean or fix something, he would plead fatigue or sickness. He would ask for medical slips and then absent himself for days at a time. When he returned he would smell of alcohol. The other Rwandese began to talk to me about him. "He is drinking," they said. Or worse, for the Rwandese: "He is *lazy*."

A few months after we had hired Benjamin, the small cash box kept in a locked drawer in our showroom was discovered missing. We calculated that a total of roughly 5,000 shillings (around $100 US) had been inside the box. It had disappeared after hours; the following morning the doors of the shop were padlocked and undisturbed. As it turned out, there was no clear evidence that any one of our employees had stolen the cash box. But of course one of them had; it was impossible for anyone else to have gotten at it. Only Michael and I had keys. Benjamin, Marie, Virginia, and Berehe immediately turned against one another, accusing one or the other of stealing.

Michael and I were furious. We felt betrayed. Not only had we hired the four, but we had provided them with meals, given them extra clothes, loaned them money, and cared for them when they were in trouble. We felt they were our friends. Now one of them had stolen from us—or more precisely, stolen from the *refugees* since this was their money. I was determined to get to the bottom of it. So, reasoning that the missing cash box would still be around, Michael and I drove to each of their houses, with Benjamin, Patricia, Virginia, and Berehe in tow, and searched for the missing cash box.

It was an agonizing affair, and one about which, even as I write these words, I am deeply embarrassed. I was probably well within my rights, as it was abundantly clear that one of them had in fact stolen the money. It was, then, the correct thing to do for *one* of them, but not for the other three. It was deeply humiliating for them; in fact I could imagine nothing more humiliating, and as I searched their small shacks, I felt ashamed. We found nothing in anyone's house. So now what?

"Fire them all," counseled a longtime American expat. "That's the only fair way. It'll send a message that you don't tolerate stealing, otherwise the refugees and the Kenyans will take advantage of you. Fire them all," he repeated lest I miss the point. "That's the way it's done here." Even the *refugees* counseled me to fire the staff; many had been visibly angered when they heard of the robbery. An Irish priest agreed. "Sack them all," he said simply.

It was an agonizing decision, but at the time it seemed the only course of action. Singling one out for dismissal would have been arbitrary. Personally, I suspected Benjamin. Michael suspected Berehe. In the end, we decided to fire them all. It was without a doubt the most difficult thing I ever had to do or would have to do during my time in Kenya.

I gathered them together and informed them of our decision. Virginia and Marie burst into tears, drying their eyes on their sleeves; Benjamin and Berehe simply hung their heads. After the meeting I walked into the bathroom, closed the door, and wept.

After a few weeks my soul was still uneasy, and it became clear to me that we had done the wrong thing. Punishing all of them may have been an ideal way to send a message to the other refugees and people living in Kangemi, but it was also patently unfair. Besides, firing a person meant condemning someone to a life of poverty; jobs were almost impossible—no, impossible—to come by. Already, though, we had hired a new person for the shop, Patricia Njeri, a Kenyan woman, who had proven to be a very conscientious worker.

In firing them all, Michael and I realized that we had made an enormous mistake. Still, both Benjamin and Berehe were lousy workers. We decided that the best course of action would now be to review the cases against them, one by one, to determine whether it was fair to have let them go.

We met with them individually. This, too, was a wrenching process, certainly more for them than for Michael and me. As for

Virginia, she wept and begged us to take her back, protesting her innocence, as she had all along. Marie was more subdued and admitted that the robbery had taken place under her watch; as the salesperson, after all, she was responsible for the cash box. Berehe offered no defense; he remained silent throughout our conversation. In the end, as there was absolutely no evidence against Virginia, we hired her back. But since Benjamin and Berehe had done so little work, we let their firings stand. Marie, who admitted that she had been responsible for the safety of the cash box, was not rehired.

But I *still* felt guilty. I knew that I had tried to address the situation as best I could, but I also knew that without work Benjamin, Berehe, and Marie would be impoverished. So trying to both assuage my guilt and provide for them, I started Marie with a business project, one that had initially brought her to our office: a hairdressing saloon. She said she was happy with this arrangement and that she held no grudge against us. "The cash box was my responsibility, Brother," she said sadly. For Berehe, we hastened arrangements with the UN for his emigration to Norway, a process that had been in the works for some time.

As for Benjamin, a few weeks after having been fired, he began visiting us again. Every day. "Please take me back," he would say and weep. But by this point I knew that even if I took him back, he would continue to be a poor worker. And, though I had no real evidence, I still suspected him as the thief.

But what could I do? I continued to give him "some little money" every week and counsel him about his problems. So Benjamin was back to where he had started. Sick, poor, jobless, and very much alone.

AS WITH MANY PROBLEMS faced in Kenya, there seemed to be no right answer. Or, whenever one did arrive at what seemed like the "right" answer, one still felt uneasy.

One reason I was so ashamed of my initial actions was that it seemed to reflect the many relationships in which I always had the upper hand. My power (the power to hire and fire, to take the most obvious example) stood in stark contrast to Benjamin's almost complete lack of it. Even if Benjamin *had* been guilty of stealing the money, I hadn't afforded him the benefit of the doubt (nor had I given it to the others, until after the damage was done). And my way of exercising that power—by firing Benjamin and rummaging through his house—was patently wrong. This I sensed even at the time, though anger prevented me from realizing it.

But even afterwards I remained uncertain about my response to Benjamin. Kenyans, refugees, and expats alike chided me for continuing to give Benjamin "handouts," averring that they only made him more dependent. But the other alternative, that is, *not* giving him money, would have condemned him to further misery. There were no jobs to be had. He had no skills. And there was no "safety net," no Social Security, no Medicare, no Medicaid in Kenya. The poor were on their own. I also felt the need for some sort of forgiveness on my part and maybe some atonement. So lacking a definite answer and beset by conflicting advice, I relied on my own intuition and what I saw as the most Christian response. Rather than perpetuating a cycle of vindictiveness and revenge, a cycle that I saw replicated in places like Rwanda, Somalia, and in the ethnic land-clashes in Kenya, I decided that the idea of forgiveness and reconciliation were more important than a sense of retributive "justice."

It was these kinds of wrenching episodes—for which there seemed to be no easy answers—that threw me increasingly to rely on prayer as one sort of response to my questions.

AS A JESUIT of course I had been praying regularly for a number of years. One hour a day (in addition to Mass) was the oft-stated but somewhat ambitious goal for Jesuits in training. But even if I wasn't able to squeeze in the daily hour of prayer, every night I prayed the *examen*, the short form of prayer set out by St. Ignatius Loyola, consisting in a sort of review of the day. The *examen* is arranged into five parts. First, you ask God to be with you. Second, you give thanks to God for the good things that happened during the day: anything really—a conversation with a friend, a refugee who had succeeded in her business, the taste of a mango, the smell of a gardenia bush as you passed by, the sight of the sun high in the sky. Third, you reviewed the day. You saw the events of the day, where you had noticed God at work, and where you might not have. (I used to think of this part as a sort of movie.) Fourth, you asked for a knowledge of what could be called, for better or worse, your "sinfulness," times when you consciously turned away from God's grace. Finally, you asked for help—for God's grace—in the following day. The *examen* was a surprisingly effective way of making me aware of God's presence, something that, if I didn't reflect on it, was often easy to miss. Following the firings at Mikono, for example, it was prayer that enabled me finally to see that my soul was still uneasy and, more importantly, that I had done the wrong thing.

As I moved through my time in Kenya, I found that my prayer changed—clearly but almost imperceptibly. Initially I had focused on loneliness, missing my friends and family. Then, laid up with mono, I prayed in an attempt to discern whether or not I should leave. At one point I became enamored of what is known as "centering prayer," the technique, influenced by Zen and other Eastern traditions, that "centers" the mind, opening it up to God, through a series of simple breathing exercises.

But, in time, my prayer was taken up almost exclusively with work. More and more the faces of the refugees became the focus of my prayer, and I tried to ask God how best to work with them and respond to their needs. This, however, was no guarantee that I would do the right thing.

My relationship with Sisi, a Ugandan refugee, was at times turbulent, though it eventually grew into one of mutual respect and friendship. Sisi is shown here during our basket-making class.

I MEET MAMA MZEE

Why, he wondered, swerving the car to avoid a dead dog, do I love this place so much? Is it because here human nature hasn't had time to disguise itself? ... Here you could love human beings nearly as God loved them, knowing the worst: you didn't love a pose, a pretty dress, a sentiment artfully assumed.

—Graham Greene, *The Heart of the Matter*

Jim Corrigan, the other young American Jesuit, ran the "medical assistance program," which provided free health care to the refugees in Nairobi. The refugees would visit a JRS office or a nearby Catholic parish and collect a slip from a JRS worker or parish volunteer. On the slip was written the refugee's name and UN identification number. The refugee would then carry the slip to a medical clinic, which would in turn check the identification number against the refugee's UN card. Medical treatment would be provided to the refugee; the slip would be mailed to JRS, which would reimburse the clinic. It was an excellent program: a way to provide health care to the refugees without handing out cash. The medical assistance program seemed airtight, eliminating any possibility for cheating. As usual, though, we had underestimated the resourcefulness of the refugees.

Sisieyira was a heavy woman, standing about five foot ten, who wore her hair brushed straight up from her forehead. Though her name was Ugandan, her people, she explained, came from Rwanda. Sisi, as she was called, was a regular visitor to the Mikono Centre and brought us multicolored straw baskets that sold briskly.

Sisi could produce baskets very quickly, and I found myself wondering if she were in fact buying them, as some of the other refugees had suggested she was. But I gave her the benefit of the doubt. Besides, I always took the refugees' accusations with a grain of salt. Marie, a Rwandese refugee who made dresses for us, one day accused Joseph Musoni, another Rwandese, who brought us batik paintings, of stealing the batiks and signing his name to them. "He is a thief," she said bluntly. I told her I would look into it.

I walked Marie out to the porch. Joseph stood up, glared at Marie as she passed, and followed me into the office.

"Ah, you know, Brother," he said conspiratorially, "This woman, this Marie, she is a cheat! She is buying her dresses from the market!"

ANOTHER WOMAN who seemed to find me an easy mark was Mama Mzee. Her nickname meant, literally, "Old Woman," but both *mama* and *mzee* were terms of great respect in Kenya. Mama Mzee was a short Sudanese woman with jet-black skin. Like Sisi, she wove beautiful baskets of all sizes, but in the Sudanese style: dried tan straw shot through with grasses dyed red, green, and black. Her basket work was so fine that we asked her to run a basket-making workshop for the other refugee women. Lessons would run for a week and be offered free to the refugees. We would pay Mama Mzee 500 shillings a week for her teaching—a princely sum. We posted signs advertising the courses, and bought thousands of shillings of supplies for Mama Mzee: straw, knives, dye, pots to boil the dye, and wood to make the fire for the pots to boil the dye, all of which we stored in our bathroom.

The course attracted twenty women who sat in the back yard weaving in the shade of a large avocado tree. We provided them with a simple meal at midday—*ugali*, the Kenyan staple of boiled white corn meal formed into a cake, and its culinary partner, *sukuma wiki*, chopped vegetable greens fried with tomatoes and onions. *Sukuma wiki* was often used as a filler, when more nourishing food was unavailable or unaffordable. Its name means, literally, "to push the week."

I was surprised to note that after the first week of classes, the women had only finished tiny circles of straw. "These students are *very* slow," said Mama Mzee dolefully. "They will need another week of school."

I hadn't imagined that it would take quite so long to make a basket. But what did I know about basket making? So I paid her 500 shillings for the first week and asked her to return. Another week passed with the women sitting in the back yard chatting and plaiting straw. This time they were only halfway done. "They are *so* slow, Brother," said Mama shaking her head. But I soon realized it was in Mama's best interest for them to progress as slowly as humanly possible. Better to be paid for three weeks than for one.

"One more week, Mama, and that's it," I said. "This is the last week for the course, whether they are finished with their baskets or not."

She considered this for a moment and agreed.

Not surprisingly, all twenty women finished their baskets in the next week. They thanked me profusely for the classes, which they loved, they said. Next they tried to sell me their baskets. I explained that since I had already purchased the materials in the first place, it was a bit much to ask me to purchase the goods as well. We settled on my paying them for their labor.

Mama Mzee, for her part, seemed to like me even *more* after my stern admonition. (It reminded me of the Christmas cup episode.) She became a regular visitor to Mikono Centre, dropping by almost daily, even if she had nothing to sell. Eventually Mama took it upon herself to inform me which refugees were going to cheat me and which were honest. She sat placidly on the porch throughout the day, arms folded, eyeing the refugees who passed through the shop. Though I never thought she was any better at gauging the truth than I was, I enjoyed her presence and grew to appreciate her blunt advice, which she offered freely. "You have a mother in the United States," she said to me one day, "but here in Africa, Mama Mzee is your mother."

SISI, WHOM MAMA MZEE had warned me about, seemed to be sick all the time and was constantly asking for medical slips, which I was happy to provide. I noticed that she also would ask for slips for her children, and so I would write out: "Sisi Mukamarasi and child" on the slip, followed by Sisi's UN identification number.

One day Sister Madeline, the White Sister who ran the clinic, or "dispensary," at St. Joseph the Worker, dropped by to visit. Did I know Sisi? she asked. Yes I did.

Sister Madeline sighed and passed her fingers through her grey hair.

Sister Madeline explained that she had caught Sisi cheating on her medical slips. Sisi, she discovered from other refugees, would ask us for a slip for her and her child. But the children she brought to the dispensary were not her own. Instead, local Kenyan women paid Sisi 50 shillings to accompany their children to the dispensary for medicine. It was an ingenious plan: Sisi's identification number would always match what was written on the slip, but the children were seen without anyone checking *their* ID cards. "But now, Brother, we shall have to check the children as well," said Sister Madeline.

But what to do about Sisi? Jim Corrigan and I decided that it would be best to confront her squarely with the accusations. We met with her together, in Jim's office across town, away from

the other refugees. When I outlined the situation, she wept loudly and howled.

"No, Brother Jim, I *cannot* be lying to you! You are my
Brother! Surely I *cannot* be cheating you!"

Unfortunately, we knew her story probably wasn't true. And
so, not only to penalize Sisi for taking advantage of the system,
but also to show other refugees that cheating would not be toler-
ated, I forbade Sisi from coming to the Mikono Centre. I knew,
of course, that this would be devastating. Where would she sell
her baskets? She howled even louder. "Oh, Brother, have *mercy* on
me!"

Every day for the next few weeks, Sisi would visit the Mikono
Centre, but I would refuse to meet with her. She would weep
outside our office, protesting her innocence, asking other refugees to support her. I knew I was supposed to be resolute about
not letting her back. ("That's the only way she'll figure out that
you're serious," another JRS worker told me.) In time, though,
my resolve weakened, and I began to pity her. Surely she had suffered enough for her small crimes, which, after all, were only
designed to help her feed herself and her children better.

Two months passed, and I told Sisi she could come back. I
figured she had learned whatever lesson she would learn. One
thing I knew for certain: the other refugees had discovered what
Sisi had done and were not going to repeat her mistake. One
episode in particular confirmed this: a young Sudanese man
asked me for a medical slip because, he said sadly, he had an
abscess on his penis. "Please look, Brother," he said, and swiftly
unbuckled his belt, dropping his trousers.

This, of course, was the very last thing I wanted to see.
"That's OK, that's OK!" I shouted, covering my eyes. "I believe
you!"

"No, Brother, I must be *showing* you!" he said. "You must
see that I am not cheating you!"

So the point had been made—perhaps too strongly. In any
event, it was time for reconciliation. The refugees had faced
enough rejection, anyway. Sisi wept when I told her to come in

and visit with me. From then on she never asked for one medical referral slip. We became friends again, and I bought dozens of her baskets.

Mama Mzee didn't like this; it not only contradicted her advice—"Never let her back!" she had said—but also interfered with her own thriving basket trade.

I reminded her that her record on fair business was far from perfect.

"What about that course you taught, Mama? Did it really have to be going on for three weeks?"

She looked shocked. "Brother Jim!" she shouted. "Mama Mzee could *never* be cheating her own child!"

THE RAINS

The country, it seemed, was going to plunge into one of those stinging drizzles that went on end-lessly. On such days the sun never said good morn-ing, or else good night. Without a watch, you could never guess the time.

—Ngugi wa Thiong'o, *A Grain of Wheat*

There are two rainy seasons in Kenya—long and short. The long rains visit the country in April, the short, around November. But between the rains, that is, for most of the year, Nairobi's weather is ideal: no humidity, clear skies, cool breezes, temperatures in the seventies during the day and into the fifties after sunset.

Nairobi lies almost directly on the equator, and the sun blazes accordingly. The altitude, which at roughly five thousand feet keeps the city comfortable, also keeps at bay much of the malaria that plagues the rest of Kenya. To that end, the British High Commissioner related to me the old chestnut that East Africa held three attractions for the British colonists: Altitude, Alcohol, and Adultery.

During the rains, though, the morning sky is a dark grey. Towering clouds fill the heavens throughout the day; torrential storms arrive in the late afternoon. Often it would rain the entire day, turning the city's dirt roads into impassable rivers of mud and choking the culverts with foaming masses of red water.

Raincoats are not used in Kenya. Instead Kenyans make do with more homey gear. Along the road to the Mikono Center was a steep incline that my jeep always struggled to master. The road afforded a beautiful view of the Ngong Hills—sometimes a pearly grey, sometimes a pale, almost translucent green, sometimes a cerulean blue. Kenyan women, bent under the weight of enormous bags of firewood strapped to their foreheads by leather thongs, walked with painful slowness up the steep hill. The Kenyan long-distance runners, familiar to marathon aficionados and Olympic fans, were there every morning, sprinting barefoot up and down the hill. (Often the jeep would fail and Olympic hopefuls would help me push it up the hill.) By the side of this road stood banks of plants with broad green leaves and thick stems. During the rains the local Kenyans plucked the leaves, turned the stems up and placed them on their heads, where they served as effective umbrellas. Others employed black garbage bags as raincoats, poking holes in the greasy bags for the head and arms. This made for some dry Kenyans but, packed together with the windows rolled up, some very smelly *matatus*.

Following the rains, Nairobi explodes with flowers and blooming trees and bushes. On the roadsides the immense jacaranda trees showcase large blossoms of an almost comically vivid lavender, like something out of a Dr. Seuss book. And as the green leaves have not yet unfurled, the bright lavender is for a few weeks the sole surprising color in its branches.

But during my two years in Kenya, the country labored under a severe drought. Such a drought, which might have been merely an annoyance to city-dwellers in Europe and the States, was for Kenyans a disaster, and occasioned great suffering. For those in much of the country, particularly in the north, there was the ever-present danger of death from dehydration. The growing numbers of deaths were reported daily in the Nairobi papers. And so the rains, when they came, were greeted with elation, particularly outside of Nairobi in the farm and tea country.

For the farmer who already lived on a thin ecological edge, a drought meant no crops, no crops meant no money, no money meant starvation. Those who made their living from animals were, during the drought, desperate to find grass for grazing. One day at the Mikono Centre, one of the refugees wandered into my office and announced, "Brother, *kuna kondoo.*"

It sounded, I thought, like he had said, "There are sheep." But I must have misunderstood.

He simply repeated himself and pointed toward the front yard. I walked onto the porch and saw a young thin Maasai boy with his herd of perhaps twenty sheep grazing on our tiny lawn. During the drought there was nowhere else for his sheep to go, the boy said forlornly. We let them eat.

JOHN MUTABURUNGA
AND HIS COWS

For sighing comes more readily to me than food,
and my groans well forth like water.

—Job 3:25

Besides helping refugees who made handicrafts
and those who qualified for small business projects, the Mikono Centre also sold goods made by
refugees who did *not* qualify for sponsorship from JRS. Since we
were charged with assisting only those refugees recognized as
such by the UN, there were many we were unable to help, but
who nonetheless needed financial assistance. To assist this group
of refugees, we simply bought their crafts and sold them, thus
providing them with a market for their goods.

Didace Kamagunga, for example, not only made embroidered dresses and shirts, but also painted oil pictures of Rwandese Madonnas. A few weeks after news of the genocide of the
Tutsi in Rwanda, Didace told me that he had a special painting
for me. "This is the Madonna of Kigali," he said. This Rwandese

Mary, on a field of royal blue, had almond-shaped eyes and wore a simple blouse and a white kerchief. The infant Jesus, carried on Mary's back in a cloth, wept.

Similarly, Mark Lutaaya, a tall, bespectacled Ugandan man who had studied art in Kampala, painted Last Suppers. In his paintings Jesus and the Apostles were depicted as slender elegant Africans, wearing Ugandan robes, seated in front of a table laden with East African foods. Mark's Last Suppers were a popular item in our shop and sold particularly well among religious communities. We brought the finished canvases for framing to a handicraft shop in town run by a Mr. H.P. Singh, a cheerful Indian fellow who worked alongside his taciturn wife. Mr. Singh, for his part, liked Mark's work so much that he ordered some for his store, providing Mark with still another market for his craft. Mark was delighted as special orders began coming in from our customers and from Mr. Singh.

One Maltese tourist admired Mark's paintings in the Mikono Centre and commissioned a large Last Supper. He gave me the dimensions over the phone. Mark worked three weeks on it.

When Mark had finished, I called the man, who said that he was leaving town and was much too busy to pick it up at the shop. Could I deliver it to his hotel?

I drove across town to the Jacaranda Hotel, where he was waiting for me, with some friends, in the parking lot. Apparently, they were about to leave for the airport. I greeted him and unrolled the large canvas, proudly displaying Mark's handiwork.

"They're black!" he said disdainfully.

"Of course they're black," I said.

"Well, I'm not going to buy *that*. I thought they'd be white."

I asked him why, exactly, he thought the figures were going to be white. All of Mark's pictures that he had seen in the shop were of Africans.

"Because *I'm* white, of course," he answered testily. "Tell him to do it over. You can mail it to me." He turned toward his friends and started away.

Excuse me, I said. I reminded him that since Mark drew his

Last Suppers in a distinctive style, it would be a little ridiculous to have white people sitting around a table clad in African robes. I also knew that Mark would be hurt if I returned the painting. When I thought of all the trouble Mark went to—and it really was a fine painting—I found the courage to stand my ground. Besides, I had driven halfway across town. I told him I expected to be paid in full. He gave me the money and muttered something to his friends in Maltese.

THE SHOP ENABLED many refugees, like Gauddy Ruzage, Didace Kamagunga, Mark Lutaaya, Alice Nabwire, and Agostino and Zechariah, to finally turn a profit. But because of the sometimes insurmountable odds that the refugees faced— sickness, hunger, police harassment—almost half of the projects failed. Still, even our American and European donor agencies recognized this as a respectable track record. In our short annual report they read a summary of the projects, which included not only the successes like Agostino and Gauddy, but also the stories of people like Specie Kantegwa and her murdered sister, underlining the stunning problems every refugee faced. But often even I was overwhelmed when I fully apprehended the depth of their difficulties.

John Mutaburunga was a middle-aged man who came from a family of cattle herders in Rwanda. Whenever he visited our office he wore a threadbare blue corduroy jacket and an old fedora covered with the red dirt that covered everything else in Nairobi. John asked us to help him buy a few cows. He told us that a friend had offered him free ground for grazing outside of the city. It seemed incredible, but since cows were cheap and grazing land in Nairobi proper was unavailable, we gave him the capital to purchase four cows, the necessary feed, and some tools.

I heard nothing from John for some months. One day, he appeared in my office, looking wan. His cows were doing poorly. "They are very thirsty," he said. Two had already died. Could I please come and see them?

The next afternoon, I drove out to meet John in Ngong, a town a few kilometers outside of Nairobi, populated primarily by Maasai herders, who strode deliberately through the dusty streets wearing their red plaid *shukas* and carrying long herding sticks over their shoulders. John waved at me from in front of a small bank.

He climbed into my jeep, and we drove over the green Ngong Hills to the other side of the plateau, where the landscape became progressively drier and dustier. Though Nairobi was almost always cool and breezy, once you ventured outside of Nairobi it became, as a friend liked to say, "Africa hot"—the very heat you imagine that Africa would offer. As we descended from the mountains the landscape opened up into the plain, with dry grasses, low bushes, and thorn trees. Impala slept in the distance, and vultures wheeled overhead in the clear sky. Hopeful Maasai women stood by the side of the road selling fresh honey in soda bottles. The dirt road was deeply rutted, and eventually enormous rocks made the road impassable, even for the sturdy jeep.

We got out of the jeep and examined the landscape. Far off in the distance was a cluster of tiny white shacks. "I live just there," said John, gesturing vaguely. Though it was late afternoon, I was astounded at the heat and asked him how he could expect to raise cattle here. He told me that this was the only land he could find. It was free and his Maasai friends allowed him to graze his cattle there. Every day he led his donkey into town and carried back two jerrycans of water. It had taken us an hour by jeep to ride to this point, and we had yet to reach his house. How long did it take him to walk back and forth with his donkey?

"Three hours, Brother. But if I had a truck I would be making the trip much faster."

It was unbelievable to think that he expected to raise cattle here. There was no water and no grass. As biting flies buzzed around us, we tried to come up with solutions to his problem: Could he take his cows elsewhere? No, he would have to pay to graze anywhere else. Perhaps he could sell the cows' milk to make a little money. No, he explained patiently, if the cows don't drink water, they don't give milk. What did his neighbors do with their cattle?

"They are Maasai. They migrate with their cows. But my family does not know how to live like that, Brother."

So we stood silently under the blazing sun and surveyed the bleak landscape. John Mutaburunga had no money to pay for a bus ticket to Rwanda, and at this point, who would choose to return? His remaining relatives, all Tutsis, were most likely dead. His wife had recently died of AIDS, leaving him with three children. He had no money. John had one talent: he knew how to raise cows. So, of course, he had asked us for cows. And John had only one place to graze, the arid land offered by his generous Maasai friends. But by following the only things that were certain in his life and working diligently, he had met with disaster. It was the plight of most of the refugees in Nairobi.

John was, I saw clearly, doomed to fail. A wave of profound and inarticulate sadness swept over me as I realized that there was little I could do for him. John wept when I told him that it would be impossible for us to buy him a truck; we simply didn't have enough money. Perhaps the best thing would be for John to sell his remaining cows before they died. "But, Brother, what will I do then?"

I didn't know, I said.

And I still don't.

THE HOME
OF THE WIND

In this decayed hole among the mountains
In the faint moonlight, the grass is singing
Over the tumbled graves, about the chapel
There is the empty chapel, only the wind's home.
—T.S. Eliot, *The Waste Land*

The largest group of refugees with whom I
worked were, from the beginning, Rwandese.
Many had settled in Nairobi in the 1960s and
1970s, following the continuing violence between the Hutu and
Tutsi, a strife which at times abated but never entirely disappeared.

Some of the Jesuits in my community were surprised to
learn of the predominance of Rwandese among the refugees. But
it made sense: the Rwandese were, by virtue of the length of time
in Kenya, the most "settled" of the refugees in the city. Newer
refugee groups, the Somalis for example, who poured into
Nairobi during my stay, first needed to settle themselves before
discovering what types of social services were available.

Early on, I mentioned this phenomenon to a friend who asked innocently, "Why are they still here? What's wrong with going home to Rwanda?" A few months later, in April of 1994, he would have his answer.

In the first few days it seemed too unbelievable to be true. Information was sketchy and incomplete. For the past few months there had been rumors of massacres in Rwanda as well as in Burundi, duly reported in the Nairobi papers but largely ignored elsewhere. At the beginning of the crisis, the *Daily Nation* simply recounted rumors heard from Kigali. CNN at the time found it difficult to obtain any accurate coverage, relying instead on telephone reports from the capital city of Kigali and footage of diplomats and expats being flown into Nairobi. This gave the rather bizarre impression that the flight of a small number of internationals was of greater importance than the genocide of an entire ethnic group. One memorable shot on CNN showed a prosperous-looking American woman leading her little dog off a Hercules transport plane at Jomo Kenyatta Airport in Nairobi.

Finally, news from the interior began trickling in. The numbers were revised and raised daily. One hundred thousand were dead, and two hundred thousand refugees had fled. Three hundred thousand were dead, and an equal number of refugees were displaced.

In time, we realized that the worst news, the most incredible, was the most accurate: eight hundred thousand were dead, with one million refugees living in camps with little water and no food. Cholera began to spread in the camps. Five thousand who had taken refuge in one church were slaughtered. Neighbors turned on one another. Kigali was nearly deserted. The rivers in Rwanda were clogged with bodies, some of which began to float into Lake Victoria. The papers published gruesome pictures of bloated corpses.

For the Rwandese refugees in Nairobi, many of whom had been patiently saving money for the time when it was safe to return home, the lack of information from their families, coupled with horrific pictures in the newspapers, was unbearable.

The change among the Rwandese refugees in Nairobi was immediately noticeable. They still visited us daily; after all, they still needed to eat and provide for themselves. Now, though, only one topic was on their lips. "What have you heard from our country?"

Most of the city's Rwandese were Tutsi, and therefore relatives of the victims of the current massacre. Of course there was no way for them to contact their families, and so they waited like the rest of the world for news. Ironically, while the diplomats fled, the Rwandese living in Nairobi seemed to want to return, driven to find out what had happened to their families. And gradually, I noticed a few of the regulars at Mikono Centre had disappeared. I am going back to look for relatives, one woman told me, saying good-bye. My husband has gone back to fight in Rwanda, said one woman sadly. Gone to train with the Rwanda Patriotic Front in Tanzania, another said.

Within weeks hundreds of Rwandese appeared in Nairobi, many having fled in advance of a massacre they had long anticipated with fear—after all, they had heard the Hutu radio broadcasts for months, urging the Hutu to kill their Tutsi neighbors. They settled in slums like Riruta and Dandora and Kawangware with relatives, friends, and with Rwandese they had met on the streets of Nairobi.

Three Rwandese Jesuit priests, well known by the Jesuits in Nairobi, were killed with *pangas*, machetes, at a retreat house in Kigali called the Centre Christus. The murderers separated the Jesuits and the retreatants—mostly priests and sisters—by ethnic group and murdered the Tutsi. Seventeen in all were killed, the very first, it was said, to be massacred in Rwanda. The rector of the Jesuit theology school in Nairobi, Augustin Karekezi, the soft-spoken Rwandese priest with whom I vacationed in Mombasa, lost most of his family in Kigali during the same week. He offered Mass for his country in the small Jesuit chapel at Hekima, standing before the large crucifixion scene. Months later Father Karekezi would leave his position at the school to return to his country to work at the Centre Christus, replacing his slain Jesuit brothers.

In his book *Christianity and the African Imagination*, Aylward Shorter, a member of the Missionaries of Africa, writes the story of Sister Félicité Niyitegeka, a Hutu, aged about sixty. She was the director of the Centre Saint Pierre in Gisenyi; it was there that she and her sisters sheltered Tutsi refugees during the genocide. When her brother, a colonel in the army, instructed Félicité to leave immediately in order to escape certain death, she wrote the following letter:

> *Dearest Brother,*
>   *Thank you for wanting to help me. I would rather die than abandon the forty-three persons for whom I am responsible. Pray for us, that we may come to God. Say "goodbye" to our old Mother and our brother. When I come to God, I shall pray for you. Keep well. Thank you for thinking of me. If God saves us, as we hope, we shall see each other tomorrow.*
>   *Your Sister, Felicitas Niyitegeka*

Félicité and her sisters continued to save dozens of people by helping them across the border. On April 21, the militia arrived at the Centre Saint Pierre and transported the remaining Tutsis, as well as Félicité and her sisters, to an already-prepared mass grave. They shot to death more than twenty refugees and six of the sisters, leaving Félicité for last. "I have no more reason to live," she said, "now that you have killed all of my sisters."

But for every story of a murdered priest or sister there came rumors, a few later substantiated, of Rwandese priests and sisters who were themselves murderers or who had acted in collusion with the *génocidaires*. Rwanda, it was noted many times, is the most Catholic country in Africa.

At the airport one day, I met a Belgian priest who had worked in Rwanda for twenty-four years in a small mission parish. We sat on a wooden bench, as dozens of UN troops, wearing their robin's-egg-blue helmets, swirled about us. He had been spirited out of his village during the massacres by the Belgian military, after remaining for as long as he could.

He told me of the leader of the small Christian community in his parish, who was also the head "catechist," that is, the lay person responsible for instructing people in Christianity. This catechist took the lead in killing people in his village. He was an effective organizer of genocide since he knew, thanks to his leadership role in the community, who were Hutu and who were Tutsi (an often difficult distinction to make). And so he led the rest of the Hutu in slaughtering his fellow parishioners with *pangas*. "This man," said my priest friend, "who I thought was the best Christian in the village." He paused and stared sadly at the pale blue helmets that encircled us.

"My life," he whispered, "has been a waste of time."

KABINA SOCKOR

We know that all things work together for good
for those who love God.

—Romans 8:29

Though we had seen few refugees from outside
of East Africa, I was not surprised when Kabina
Sockor, a refugee from Liberia, turned up on our
porch one morning. Some surprising comments offered by the
occasional refugee made me realize that the Mikono Centre had
become well known in Nairobi. The grapevine let people know
what we were doing. I mentioned this to Sister Luise one day.
She laughed. "I told you, Brother! There are one hundred thousand refugees in Nairobi, and now they *all* know where you are."

Kabina was a young man, who on the day of our first meeting wore a dirty T-shirt, faded grey polyester pants, and thin-
soled sandals. His story, as he related it, was incredible. Unlike
the story of Kiiza, the Ugandan man abducted by the Kenyan
police, there were no fellow refugees to corroborate his tale.
Instead Kabina showed me a torn, creased article detailing his
story that had appeared in a magazine in Liberia after his escape.

Kabina's older brother had been an officer in one of the government ministries in Liberia. As such, Kabina was strongly identified with one political party. During a flare-up of political hostilities in Liberia, his brother was abducted by members of a rival party. While Kabina watched, his brother was buried alive with other members of his party. "We will do the same to you," they told him, "unless you leave."

Kabina decided to flee Liberia, leaving behind—as all refugees do—his family, his friends, his job, his home. He first traveled to Côte d'Ivoire, which borders Liberia, settling there as an official "full status" UN refugee. But after lodging with some Liberian refugees for a few months, Kabina heard rumors that Liberian soldiers were searching for him. Apparently the political strife in his country had not yet subsided, and Kabina was still in danger. His friends advised him to get as far away from Liberia as possible. So he left Côte d'Ivoire first for Kinshasa, thousands of kilometers away in Zaire (now Congo), by jumping on and off trucks, or "lorries." Lorry travel is quite common among refugees, as the lorries are one of the few reliable and cheap ways—in addition to walking—of traveling across the continent. Finally, he ended up in Kampala, Uganda. But there were no Liberians in Uganda, and Kabina grew lonely and sad.

Kabina also discovered that the UN would give him no help in any country other than Côte d'Ivoire. To discourage refugees from wandering from country to country in search of a better deal, the UN grants papers and status forms to refugees only in their *first* country of asylum. In every other country he was *persona non grata*.

Eventually Kabina learned that lorries made frequent runs between Kampala and Nairobi. This was, in fact, one of the prime ways that the AIDS virus was initially spread through East Africa—by lorry drivers who carried the disease from Uganda. And so fearing for his life in Liberia, anxious in Côte d'Ivoire, and despairing of his treatment in Kampala, Kabina headed for Nairobi, where he had heard there were many Liberian refugees and which was far from Liberia and his brother's killers.

But in Nairobi Kabina found only more misery. There were in fact very few refugees from Liberia, he was not permitted to remain legally in the country, and he had absolutely no money. He had been reduced to begging and scrounging through garbage cans for food.

Kabina reached the end of the story and stared at me with bloodshot eyes. "Is this the place where people can start businesses?" he asked.

He reached into his dirty pants pocket, and pulled out a creased photo. It showed Kabina lounging on a concrete floor against a red oxide wall, wearing a pair of orange and green *kitenge* pants. "I made those pants, Brother," he said. "And I can make anything. Can I have a sewing machine?"

Unfortunately, the charter of JRS prohibited us from sponsoring refugees without UN papers. It was a good rule: it helped to ensure that we helped only people who were truly refugees. In this case, though, it was working against someone in need who was a real refugee.

But in a striking example of coincidence or God's providence, depending on one's beliefs (mine was definitely the latter in this case), we were able to help Kabina.

MIKONO CENTRE HAD by now become a clearinghouse and meeting place for the refugees. People taped letters for one another on outside walls and caught up on news while sitting on the long benches on the porch. Fearful of robberies and lacking storage space in their cramped houses, the refugees also asked us to store things for them: fabric, clothes, wood for carving, straw for baskets.

One day, Adela, a Rwandese refugee who made a good living by doing tailoring and mending in her house in Kawangware, appeared at our shop with her Singer 241N sewing machine, heavy table and all. At first I thought it might be broken. It was not.

She stood when she saw me. "Brother," she said, holding her hands out. "My house has been burned down! These thieves have taken everything and all I have is my machine!" As the other refugees on the benches listened to her story, Adela wept. She had lugged the heavy machine from her house over the muddy fields, a distance of about five kilometers. "Brother, can I be keeping my machine here until I get a new place?"

It was an easy request to grant. We dragged the heavy machine inside. Adela shook my hand vigorously and said she felt better now that her machine was safe. I agreed to keep it until she found a new flat, or longer if she felt it was still unsafe. "Maybe others will need it," Adela said as she left. "They can be using it, too."

Now someone did. Since we couldn't sponsor Kabina directly, I asked if he would be willing to make some caps for us with Adela's machine. We already had dozens of bolts of vividly colored batik fabric—one of our biggest sellers—made by two industrious Rwandese women with the euphonious names of Immaculate Murakatete and Edith Kabaganwa. I brought Kabina into the main showroom; together we selected some suitable fabric. We dragged Adela's machine out of the little bathroom, which was— owing to piles of small ebony logs and three large bales of straw— now more of a storage room than a bathroom.

Kabina set to work in our back yard under the avocado tree. In a few hours he presented me with three batik *kofias*, hats. They were well done; I paid him 200 shillings, his first income in weeks.

Thereafter Kabina visited us daily, selected fabric, and sewed for us on Adela's machine. After a few weeks, he had earned enough money to rent a small flat. After a few months, he was able to purchase his own machine and started doing light tailoring for his neighbors.

MY BROTHER

If you always imagine God in the same way, no
matter how true and beautiful it may be, you will
not be able to receive the gift of the new ways he
has ready for you.

—Carlos Valles, S.J., *Sketches of God*

After two years I had decided—along with my
Jesuit superiors—that the time had come to
return home. Though I loved the work (and my
father had by now recovered from his stroke), my original commitment had been completed, and I felt it was the right time
to leave.

Though I had told the refugees all along that I would be
working with them for only two years, I wanted to give them time
to get used to the idea. Their lives were replete with departures,
transitory friendships, and impermanence. So a few months
before my departure I put up a note on the window of the
Mikono Centre, in English, Swahili, French, Amharic, Luganda,
and Kinyarwanda. It explained the reason for my departure—
continuing my studies for ordination in the States—and assured

them of the continued support of JRS for themselves and their businesses.

Posting the note in the window also occasioned the expression of good wishes and affection from the refugees. Some brought me notes, some carried gifts, and others brought their children and parents for me to say good-bye to and bless. All of this I was quite unprepared for and found tremendously affecting. My JRS colleagues also planned a going-away party to be held in the back yard of the Mikono Centre, similar to our Christmas party.

"Will there be any more cups, Brother?" someone asked.

LEAVING ALSO AWAKENED in me a need to reconcile myself with Marie Bugwiza and Benjamin, two of the people Michael and I had fired. The third man, Berehe, the Ethiopian refugee, had by this point been successfully resettled in Norway. The passage of time only served to increase my regret about my actions. So one day I sat down with Marie Bugwiza and told her bluntly that I was sorry for any heartache that I caused her. Marie nodded her head as I spoke and interrupted me before I could finish. "You had no choice, Brother." She was, she explained, no longer sad, and she appreciated our support in the new project. My meeting with Benjamin was more difficult, as he was still poor and still looking for work. I told him how sorry I was, how I wished him well still, and how I would continue to pray for him. This may have been cold comfort to him, but I hoped that he saw that I had all along tried to do the right thing for him. But was it enough?

A FEW DAYS AFTER THE NOTE was posted, Michael told me that Kabina Sockor was waiting on the porch to see me.

His face was wet with tears as he entered the small office where I met with refugees. I was surprised; not only do African men rarely weep in public, but I also knew that Kabina had had a difficult life—perhaps I expected him to be "tough." I closed the door.

After he sat down and wiped his eyes on his sleeve, I asked him what was wrong.

"You're leaving," he said.

His words made me think that he was worried about what things would be like after I had left. So I quickly reassured him, reminding him that Brother Michael would continue to work here and that the Mikono Centre would continue to help him out.

He lowered his head. "No, Brother. You are not understanding."

And so I again attempted to reassure him. "You know," I said, "even though things have been difficult for you, people here will take care of you. And you've come so far. You've got a flat, your own tailoring business. There's no reason to think that things can't continue to improve for you."

"You are still not understanding, Brother," he said. His head sank and he closed his eyes. Tears dropped onto his jacket.

Kabina reached over and grabbed my arm. We were sitting next to one another, on low wooden chairs with cushions. He turned his damp face to mine.

"You're my brother," he said.

And I understood. I understood exactly what he meant. Of course, I had heard the gospel stories where Jesus says that we are all brothers and sisters, that we're all part of the Body of Christ, that "no man is an island," and all of that, but I never really understood it before. Now I understood. I *was* Kabina's brother. And he was mine. I was responsible for him, to help him out, to be his friend. By virtue of our time together and our concern for one another, we were truly brothers. Now tears filled my own eyes.

"Yes, I am. And you're mine," I said, finally.

"WHEN ARE YOU COMING BACK, BROTHER?"

As I stood and looked at them a fancy came back to me that had taken hold of me before: It was not I who was going away, I did not have it in my power to leave Africa, but it was the country that was slowly and gravely withdrawing from me, like the sea in ebb-tide.

—Isak Dinesen, *Out of Africa*

The day of the farewell party, April 15, began with the sun shining bright in the intense blue Kenyan sky. Michael had made the preparations, along with Virginia and Patricia, our assistants at Mikono Centre. Uta, who had recently returned with Jürgen from Germany, arrived early with Sister Luise and Father Eugene. John Guiney and the parish staff from St. Joseph the Worker were there, too, along with Sister Madeline and the White Sisters, as well as a

In a photo taken toward the end of my stay, my colleagues and I pose at the entrance to the Mikono Centre on a cool and cloudy morning. Pictured with me are (clockwise) a novice from the Loretto Sisters novitiate (who dropped by as we were taking the picture), Patricia Njeri, Michael Schöpf, and Virginia Gatonye.

number of Jesuits from my community, and my American friends.

Many refugees came bearing gifts that they had made. All things that I had seen a hundred times before, of course: rugs, baskets, wooden animals, shirts, fabrics, batiks, but now with a twist. Sarah Nakate, the Ugandan woman who made tablecloths and napkins, brought me a gift, that she said represented America and Africa. "Your two homes, Brother." On the long side of the tablecloth Sarah had embroidered baboons, on the short side, a Native American with a feather in his head astride a horse. Africa and America.

Mama Mzee presented me with a red and green basket. "For your mother in America," she said solemnly, "from your mother in Africa."

We had cakes from the Engabire Bakery, orange Fantas, and some Ethiopian food that one of the "Blue Nile" Ethiopian restaurants had prepared. And since this was East Africa, there were many formal speeches delivered by the refugees, songs, more speeches, stories, and finally, more speeches. Gauddy Ruzage, Kedress Kanzaire, Josée Mukagaga, Specie Kantegwa, Marie Bugwiza, and dozens of other Rwandese women, clad in formal *kitenge* skirts, stood on the lawn and sang what they announced was a special "song of farewell" from Rwanda. Given the recent genocide in Rwanda their song was especially poignant; I wondered how many times they had never gotten the chance to say farewell to people they knew far better than me.

At the end of the day I gave a speech in English and Swahili, thanking everyone and letting them know that I wouldn't forget them. Quite suddenly the sky grew dark, and it began to rain, which everyone assured me was indeed a *baraka,* a blessing.

When everyone finally took their leave, I was disconsolate. "When are you coming back, Brother?" I heard over and over, from Ugandans, Rwandese, Ethiopians, Eritreans, Sudanese, Mozambiquans, and Kenyans. It was difficult to tell them that I didn't know, but that I hoped some day soon. Gauddy made me promise to come back; Alice Nabwire said that she would not stop praying for me; Kabina Sockor asked me the name of the Jesuit superior to whom he could write, in order to assure my return. They hugged and bowed and curtsied and shook my hand and finally disappeared, clutching Fanta bottles and pieces of cake wrapped in paper napkins, dodging raindrops, back to their homes in the slums of Nairobi.

After I collected their gifts and loaded them up in the jeep, a rainbow came out in the indigo sky. I took it as a sign. Of what I'm not sure—maybe of God's covenant and promise to look after the refugees, or maybe just of God's love for them, and for me. Of course I'm aware that this coda probably sounds too perfect, too neat an ending for my time in Kenya to be even remotely true, but as the refugees would undoubtedly say: "Surely, Brother, I *cannot* be making this up."

THE MUSTARD SEED

You shall not wrong or oppress the alien,
for you were once aliens yourselves,
in the land of Egypt.

—*Exodus 22:20*

A few weeks after I returned to the States, the horrific news of the genocide in Rwanda began to dominate the media's attention. Every day brought new pictures, new reports of slaughter, and more insistent pleas for help from the world community. One day I watched television footage of the Tutsi refugees in a camp across the Zairian border. I caught the briefest glimpse of a thin young Rwandese boy huddled under a blanket, the kind of cheap blanket that is sold everywhere in Nairobi, made of multicolored pressed fabric scraps. The kind of blanket, in fact, that I had on my own bed in Nairobi. It was a strange moment; I felt at once painfully separated from this boy and profoundly connected.

SO NOW, A FEW YEARS after I left Kenya, I still meet the refugees—though in different ways. I no longer find them waiting for me by the dozens in the cool Kenyan morning, nor do I jump into my noisy jeep to visit them at home, nor do they flag me down by the side of dusty roads. Instead, I meet them in letters, in prayer, and in memory.

Some of the refugees have turned out to be surprisingly good correspondents. Alice Nabwire is pushing on with her tailoring shop in Ngando, though business is slower than she would like. Agostino's carvings remain very popular with customers at the Mikono Centre, and he tells me that he has recently sold three of his trees of life. Edith Kabaganwa writes about her batik business and the problems that she faced trying to visit her family in Rwanda. Life is still difficult for Specie Kantegwa, and she still cares for her late sister's child.

Benjamin writes almost monthly asking for "some little money." He is still sick, suffering from stomach ulcers, and desperate to find work. His life is exceedingly difficult. Mama Mzee says she is still struggling; her baskets are not selling as well as she hoped and could I please help her with this? Elizabeth Nakyobe, who has moved to Tanzania, and Irene Mukasa write to tell me about their sons, both named Jimmy. They are growing quickly. Usually their letters are accompanied by a creased photograph and a request for a photo in return. And when I am coming back to see them?

Still their letters are written on crumpled, lined paper, dictated to a scribe, and begin in the same familiar way. "Dear Brother Jim, I greet you in the name of our Lord Jesus Christ...." And I write them back, trying to offer the same type of encouragement that I did when I sat across from them, occasionally enclosing a ten or twenty dollar bill, which I know may or may not reach them.

A few of the refugees have moved on, or "shifted" as the East Africans say, in search of better circumstances. Kabina Sockor took his earnings and moved to Tanzania to set up a tailoring shop for himself. Marie Gloriosa Bugwiza has moved back to Rwanda, where she lives with her family. Many of the Rwandese refugees, in fact, journeyed home in a continuing effort to find their families. Gauddy Ruzage was away for months, I was told, in an unsuccessful search for some of her relatives.

Some of the refugees have met with great misery, like Halima Mutebe, who ran the Agali Awamu group. She, I have heard, had been jailed and tortured by the Kenyan police. A few of the refugees with whom I worked have died. Mary Kabiito, the energetic Ugandan woman who embroidered barkcloth and brought us painted leather bags, died from an AIDS-related illness the year after I left. This news was mentioned in passing in a letter sent to me by a Jesuit who happened to be passing through Nairobi.

But most of the refugees I do not hear from. Some cannot write. Some do not have enough money for paper or postage. Most of the refugees, of course, are busy enough looking for work, trying to stay healthy, making sure that they have enough money for rent and food for their children. Some are simply impossible to contact, as they cannot afford the monthly fee for a post office box and certainly have no "address" in the slums. So many of the refugees who I saw weekly, whose lives and families I was intimately familiar with, I know I will never meet or hear from again.

A FEW THINGS I KNOW now that I didn't then. For one thing, I understand that my own struggles—my brief sickness, my worries about my parents, my frustrations in my work— broke open my heart and enabled me to connect with the refugees on a deeper level. I suppose that if I had felt completely in control of things, I might not have experienced the love from the refugees so profoundly, nor have been able to love them as fully. In my weakness, then, I was more able, I think, to meet them as brothers and sisters—as friends. "In my weakness I am strong," said St. Paul. Maybe this is something of what he meant.

It is also clear that the refugees taught me how to love in a new way. One of the challenges of religious life, at least for me, has been learning what chastity means. And I think that it wasn't until I was in Kenya, spending time with people like Kabina Sockor and Gauddy Ruzage and Alice Nabwire and even Benjamin Mugabo, that I understood how satisfying it can be to love chastely, that is, to love many people with your whole heart and to accept the love that comes freely in return. Come to think of it, that's the challenge for any sort of life, religious or not.

I also know how connected we remain—still—through the miles and with the passage of time. And I know that if I am connected to my refugee friends thousands of miles away, then I am also connected to the refugee boy huddled under the blanket, that is, to a person I've never met. And, if this is true, then I'm connected to everyone else in the world. So this I know.

But there are some things I still don't know. I don't know how I should have responded to Benjamin. And I don't know what I should have told John Mutaburunga, who asked, "What will I do now?" as we stood in the blazing sun contemplating his failed dairy business. I don't know why the poor, who work so hard and suffer so much, are often rewarded only by more hardship and ever more pain.

I also, though, understand that in confronting these painful experiences during my time in Kenya, I met God. It was in facing hardships that the refugees showed me the value of something else, something good—that is, hope. It was this hope that gave their work such meaning and value, and, I believe, enabled the refugees to push on—*pole, pole* as they would say. It was this hope that they passed on to me during my time in East Africa. And the source and ground of this hope, I know, is God.

"The reign of God is like a mustard seed," said Jesus. "When sown upon the ground it is the smallest of all seeds, but when it has grown it is the greatest of all the bushes, and becomes a tree, so that the birds of the air come and make nests in its branches." So while the refugees' hope is a small thing, perhaps covered by the dirt of genocide and poverty and despair, I also know that it is there, dormant, awaiting water, but always ready to sprout forth with new life.

The refugees with whom I worked still accompany me. I close my eyes and remember them when I pray. I hear their voices; I see their faces; I think of their sorrows and their joys; I remember their hope. And I am very grateful.

ACKNOWLEDGMENTS

> In Africa people learn to serve each other. They live on credit balances of little favours that they give and may, one day, ask to have returned. In any country almost empty of men, "love thy neighbor" is less a pious injunction than a rule for survival. If you meet one in trouble, you stop—another time he may stop for you.
>
> —Beryl Markham, *West with the Night*

IN ADDITION TO THE PEOPLE whose stories are told in this book, many other good friends helped to make my work in East Africa decidedly more enjoyable. The Jesuit community at Loyola House in Nairobi made me feel welcome from the morning of my arrival; and my two religious superiors, Jonathan Haschka, S.J., and Victor Jaccarini, S.J., were always enormously understanding. (It fell to Jonathan to take his life in his hands and teach me how to drive.) George Drury, S.J., my spiritual director, was of immeasurable help, and his gracious community at Mwangaza Retreat House in Karen provided me with needed respites from a hectic work schedule. John Guiney,

S.J., Deusdedit Byabarilo, S.J., and the community at St. Joseph the Worker Parish in Kangemi helped daily with the running of the Mikono Centre, enabling me to face the various *shidas* with something resembling sanity. Thanks, too, to Tony DeSouza, S.J., and Jim Mattaliano, S.J., and the rest of the community at Holy Family Basilica for their hospitality.

Mike and Jacinta Dixon and their family offered an abundance of warm Irish hospitality by opening their home in Karen for me many times. Domatila Kieti showed me, by inviting me to her home in Kangemi, what Kenyan hospitality means. And—in case I had forgotten—the Baumann family (Betty, Bill, and Emil) and the Beltzes (Lisa and Brendan) reminded me what American hospitality meant. Thanks also to my parents, James and Eleanor Martin, and my sister and brother-in-law, Carolyn and Charles Buscarino, for being diligent correspondents during my two-year time away from home, and for the packages and gifts that would occasionally make their way through customs.

Thanks also to Mark Raper, S.J., the director of the Jesuit Refugee Service in Rome, for his support of my work in Nairobi and to Jim Lafontaine, S.J., my Jesuit superior in Boston, for his.

AS FOR THE MANUSCRIPT itself, two Jesuit friends, Steve Katsouros, S.J., and Matt Cassidy, S.J., read an early draft and offered helpful suggestions and emendations. Another two friends, Greg White and Tim Longman, are (fortunately for me) political scientists who specialize in the politics of the continent of Africa. They reviewed drafts of the manuscript as well, with an eye to ensuring its historical accuracy. Tim, a scholar of church-state relations in Rwanda and Burundi, was of particular help in my discussion of the situation in Rwanda and the plight of the Rwandese refugees in Nairobi. Mr. Casely Essamuah, a Ghanaian theologian, also read an early draft, and offered an "African" perspective on my writing. And Father Huberti Akhweso, a Tanzanian priest, corrected a good deal of poorly remembered Swahili.

Two colleagues from East Africa reviewed the manuscript to

ensure that my memory was accurate: Jim Corrigan and Sister Maddy Tiberii, S.S.J. Also, Greg Darr and Kevin Mestrich, two of the Maryknoll lay missioners in Nairobi, carefully read the final manuscript and pointed out changes that needed to be made. Kevin, who wrote his comments while still working in Nairobi, offered comments about the phenomenon of AIDS in Kenya that were invaluable for my discussion of that topic. John Conway, M.M., and Joe Healy, M.M. (both Maryknoll fathers) helped to ensure that my Swahili proverbs were remembered correctly. I am also grateful to Aylward Shorter, M. Afr., (you know—the White Fathers) for permission to quote from his fine book *Christianity and the African Imagination.*

Thanks to Jeremy Langford for his unflagging enthusiasm, support, and insightful suggestions on the original manuscript. Likewise, Eric Major, Joan Golan, and Mara Naselli provided me with ways of improving the overall structure of the book. Sister Meg Guider, O.S.F., a professor at Weston Jesuit School of Theology in Cambridge, Mass., encouraged me to reflect more deeply on some of the episodes included in this book, particularly my relationships with the refugees. Her astute comments and wise observations were exceedingly helpful. Ross Pribyl, S.J., reviewed the manuscript in its later stages, providing a wonderfully organized, page-by-page commentary. My sister Carolyn also proved to be an unexpectedly good editor. Thanks, too, go to Bob Schlichtig, S.J., and Ned Mattimoe, S.J., for their patient typing.

I am also most grateful to Robert Coles for his gracious foreword, and to Michael Coyne and Don Doll, S.J., for allowing me to use their wonderful photographs. Michael Mullins of JRS/Rome also searched his archives for suitable photos of the work of JRS in East Africa. And thanks to Liz O'Keefe for the beautiful design of this book

Finally, it is impossible to express fully my gratitude for the generosity of my refugee friends. It was a privilege and grace to work with them. This is their book.

GLOSSARY

Though the Swahili terms used in this book are defined after each use, I thought a glossary that included some fuller definitions of the terms that appear more than once would be helpful.

askari. (as-*kar*-ee) Guard or, especially, a night watchman. *Askari* was also the term used for members of the Kenyan army. Many of the night *askaris* in Nairobi were young Maasai men.

baraka. A blessing, from the verb *kubariki.*

boma. A fence. *Boma* usually refers to the thorn-bush fences used by the Maasai and other East African groups to encircle their small villages.

bwana. Though this word suffers from the pejorative Tarzan-movie stereotype of a greeting reserved for white colonials, it is actually a standard and polite term for all men, similar to "sir" or "Mister." *Jambo Bwana!* is a common Kenyan salutation.

fundi. A skilled workman. One could be a *fundi,* a sort of all-purpose handyman or more specifically, say, a *fundi wa stima,* an electrician.

hakuna. There is not, as in *hakuna shida* or *hakuna matata* (both meaning "there is no problem").

haraka. (ha-*ra*-kah) Fast. *Haraka haraka* is "very fast" and can also be used as a command, as in "hurry up." Thus the expression *Haraka haraka, haina baraka:* Hurry, hurry, means no blessings.

Hodi? Karibu! The first word means, roughly, "May I enter?" the second, "Come in" or "You are welcome!" Where Americans would respond simply "Welcome!" to "May I enter?" East Africans use the longer British form, which in the States normally implies a response to "Thank you." *Hodi?* and *Karibu* are considered the polite way to enter a house or room.

Jambo. The common greeting that means, literally, "problem?" though that meaning is normally not implied today. The response is either *Jambo*, or, if one wants to infer the actual meaning: *Nyingi*, many. *Jambo sana* (very) is used as well.

kali. Fierce. Can refer to a person (Sister Bernadette was said to be *mkali*), an animal (signs for *Mbwa Mkali*, "Fierce dog" are everywhere in Nairobi), or an object (one worked in the *jua kali*, the fierce sun, and those who worked for themselves outdoors, cutting hair, cutting wood, etc., were referred to as *jua kali* workers).

khanga. Simple, inexpensive lengths of cloth, usually patterned with geometric designs surrounded by a Swahili slogan. *Khangas* were used as wraparound skirts and as aprons. Often special *khangas* would be printed, for example, to commemorate a national holiday or, in one case, a papal visit.

kikoi. Knitted woolen fabric used traditionally by men (particularly in Somali and northern and western Kenya) and worn wrapped around the waist (in lieu of pants). Most come from artisans in Lamu, on the Kenyan coast. The *kikoi* is lightweight and traditionally striped in red or violet. Smaller ones are worn around the neck as protection against the sometimes chilly Nairobi air.

kitenge. (kee-*ten*-gay) Brilliantly colored fabrics typically made in Congo (formerly Zaire). Imported into Nairobi, these heavy cotton fabrics are highly prized for women's dresses and men's shirts and often feature striking patterns of fruits, birds, or geometric designs.

kuna. There is, as in *kuna shida* (there's a problem). The opposite is *hakuna* or *haina.*

mama. The term is used not only to refer to one's mother, but to any mature woman. *Jambo Mama!* is a perfectly polite greeting.

matatu. (ma-*ta*-tu) A minibus or a large taxi, from the Swahili *mapesa matatu*, three shillings—the original fare. *Matatus* are everywhere in Nairobi, and, at one shilling less than the city buses, are the preferred form of transportation. As drivers are paid by the mile, they speed with abandon through the crowded city streets. The small station wagons that ply their trade between the Kenyan and Tanzanian borders are also referred to as *matatus.*

mikono. (mi-*kon*-o) Hands. Plural of *mkono.*

mzee (m-*zay*). The Swahili word for "old," though it is a term of great dignity. To call a man or woman *mzee* connotes great respect.

mzungu. The easiest way to define this term is "white person." Its provenance is difficult to ascertain. One British dictionary lists it as a "clever person" though I think this was generous at best, self-serving at worst. Some Kenyans told me it meant "roundabout," and referred not only to British traffic roundabouts, but also to the colonials' often "roundabout" way of thinking. Similarly, *kizungu* is a general term for the language of whites, and is distinct from, say, *kingereza*, that is, English.

pole (*poh*-lay). An all-purpose "sorry" that can be used in almost any occasion— from the smallest inconvenience (stubbing your toe, losing a pencil) to an enormous tragedy (the death of a loved one, for example). Also, *pole sana*, very sorry. Interestingly, *pole pole* means "slow down."

posho. A boiled porridge of corn (maize) or cassava meal, more common in western Kenya and Uganda.

rungu. The Maasai fighting club, about two feet long with a knobbed end. The British refer to it as a "knobkerry." Usually carried through a leather belt or cincture.

shamba. A small plot of cultivated land. One's *shamba* can be as small as a few square feet behind one's rural home or a self-sustaining farm. Many Nairobi residents speak of their family homes in the country as their *shambas.*

shida. A problem, also a *matata.*

shuka. Many Maasai men and women wear this sort of traditional wrap. In the past, clothing consisted mainly of tanned animal hides, but with the advent of European trading to East Africa, the Maasai began to prefer brightly colored, usually plaid, lengths of cloth, which are worn wrapped around the waist and over the shoulder. Men wear a bright red, women a royal blue.

sukuma. Also known as *sukuma wiki*, a name which means literally "push the week," or a filler. *Sukuma*, an omnipresent Kenyan specialty, is usually made with a local leafy green, resembling collard greens, prepared fried with diced tomatoes and onions. It is almost invariably served with *ugali.*

tunaendelea. (tuna-en-de-*lay*-ah) We continue, from the verb *kuenda*, to go. The expression *Tunaendelea pole pole* ("We continue on slowly, slowly") was a common one. When speaking English, though, the refugees' expression was: "We push on slowly, slowly."

ugali. The Kenyan staple of white corn meal. The meal is boiled until it thickens and then sits until it forms a cake-like consistency. In this way it is similar in taste and texture to Italian dish *polenta*. It is usually served hot, often with *sukuma.*

Michael Coyne, courtesy JRS

James Martin, S.J., is associate editor of *America*, the national Catholic magazine, and editor of the book *How Can I Find God?* (Liguori/Triumph). Before entering the Jesuits, Mr. Martin, a graduate of the University of Pennsylvania's Wharton School of Business, worked for six years in corporate finance and human resources in New York City. As part of his Jesuit training, he studied philosophy and theology and, in addition to his ministry in Nairobi, has worked in a variety of settings: at a hospice for the dying in Kingston, Jamaica, with street gangs in inner-city Chicago, and as a prison chaplain in Boston. In 1998 Mr. Martin completed his master's degrees in divinity and in theology at the Weston Jesuit School of Theology in Cambridge, Mass. He will be ordained a priest in 1999.